MW01483514

THE NAKED PUN

THE NAKED PUN

FROM THE FILES

OF

GUS SILBER

WITH ILLUSTRATIONS BY
ANTHONY STIDOLPH

PENGUIN BOOKS

PENGUIN BOOKS

Published by the Penguin Group
27 Wrights Lane, London W8 5TZ, England
Viking Penguin, a division of Penguin Books USA Inc, 375
Hudson Street, New York, New York 10014, USA
Penguin Books Australia Ltd, Ringwood, Victoria, Australia
Penguin Books Canada Ltd, 10 Alcorn Avenue, Toronto, Ontario,
Canada M4V 3B2
Penguin Books (NZ) Ltd, 182-190 Wairau Road, Auckland 10, New
Zealand
Penguin Books, Amethyst Street, Theta Ext 1, Johannesburg,
South Africa

Penguin Books Ltd, Registered Offices: Harmondsworth, Middle-
sex, England

First published by Penguin Books 1994

ISBN 0 140 24660 6

Typeset by Iskova Image Setting
Printed and bound by Creda Press
Cover designed by Graphicor

CONTENTS

TRUE STORIES

OPINION

ACKNOWLEDGEMENTS

CELEBRITY FOREWORD

I have often wondered what my husband (Gus Silber) does in his study all night. Sometimes things are so quiet in there, you could hear a pun drop. But whenever I get up at three o'clock in the morning to ask him, he just says, 'Go back to sleep. I'm busy.'

When I ask him, 'busy doing what', his reply is always the same. 'Busy trying to write the foreword to my new book.'

'Oh,' I always say, 'what is it?' To which he always replies, 'Well, it's a kind of introductory statement or preface to a book.'

'Yes,' I always answer, gritting my teeth, 'I know that. What I mean is, what book is it that you're trying to write the foreword to?'

'Oh!' he always exclaims. 'Thanks for asking. Actually, it's a collection of articles, columns, and features I've written for a variety of newspapers and magazines over the years, on subjects ranging from . . .'

'Well,' I always interrupt, 'if that's the case, why don't you just use a foreword you've already written?' Then I go back to sleep. This has been going on for so long now, that I am beginning to wonder if my husband will ever complete the foreword in time.

According to his production schedule, and the growing collection of politely furious messages on his telephone answering-machine, the foreword was supposed to have been handed in several weeks ago, or months by the time you read this. Things are getting so desperate, that just yesterday (or several days ago, by the time you read this), I asked my husband why he doesn't simply do what other authors do, and get someone else to write the foreword.

After all, after almost 20 years in journalism, he must surely have built up a vast network of friends, colleagues, acquaintances, and influential contacts in various fields, and surely one of them, preferably someone famous and well known to the public at large, would be only too pleased to say a few words at the beginning of this book. He said that was a good idea, and he would give it some serious thought.

All that remains, therefore, is for me to declare this book well and truly open, and to say that I hope you enjoy reading it as much as I enjoyed writing the foreword. There, that wasn't so difficult, was it?

Amanda Silber
Author's wife
Johannesburg

HUMOUR

EXCUSE ME, HAS ANYBODY SEEN MY PEN?

I have a question. Why do pens keep disappearing? I ask because I can never find a pen when I need one, such as this very instant. Just an ordinary pen. That's all. Nothing fancy or gold-plated or platinum-nibbed or tungsten-coated or engraved along the side for 25 years' outstanding service.

Just something that, when you hold it between your thumb and index finger, and you point it at a piece of paper and wiggle your wrist a bit, it writes. A pen. You heard me. Green, black, blue, red, purple, it doesn't matter.

I'll even take one of those fat pens with five different-coloured points that all come out at the same time if you push very hard on the buttons at the top. I used to have one of those pens once. It disappeared.

I took it out of the box and I signed my name a few times in five different colours, and poof — I never saw it again. In a split-second, it joined all the other thousands of pens that have slipped through my fingers after the most fleeting of acquaintances. Pens disappear. This is a solid, scientific fact.

I have been in the business of writing things down for 15 years now, and in all that time, I have never met one other person in the same business who was able to hold on to a pen for longer than it takes to say, 'Excuse me, can I borrow your pen?'

The answer must always be 'No', because there is convincing evidence to suggest that pens disappear up to 3,5 times quicker when lent to somebody whose pen has already disappeared. The fact is, Unexplained Pen Disappearance, or 'UPD', is a worldwide phenomenon of such increasing magnitude, that it makes the disappearance of ships and planes over the Bermuda Triangle look petty.

Many investigators go so far as to say that the Bermuda Triangle itself is full of pens, many of which people could have sworn were on their desks only a second ago.

This theory was reinforced some months ago when a US Navy diver, Flight-Lieutenant Jim Penman, was exploring a small square of the Bermuda Triangle in search of a giant battleship, a nuclear submarine, three aeroplanes, and a crate of Jack Daniels that had disappeared without trace the day before.

Instead, 350 metres below the raging surface of the Atlantic Ocean, Flight-Lieutenant Jim Penman found a pen. It was a 1973 model Bic Rollerball, with a slightly nibbled top, a three-quarter reservoir of light blue ink, and a colony of approximately 15 small barnacles attached to the barrel.

Amazingly, when brought to the surface, it wrote first time. However, the incident has not been recorded in official US Navy records, because just as Flight-Lieutenant Jim Penman was about to jot down the details in his log-book, the pen disappeared.

Another theory relating to UPD, or 'Unexplained Pen Disappearance', is that pens, because of their unique molecular construction — one part carbon to two parts polyurethane and not enough ink — have a tendency to 'deconstruct' when exposed to too much oxygen.

An example of too much oxygen would be the level commonly found in your office, your home, your car, your bank, your nearest shopping centre, or anywhere else where you would normally use a pen if you were able to find one.

A chance discovery in the legendary Lost Pens section of the
Bermuda Triangle

'Pens, as a rule, operate at their optimum level of efficiency when the volume of air around them is no greater than 300 micrograms per square millimetre,' explained Professor Bill Inkman of the Department of Applied Penology at the University of Pennsylvania. 'Because of this, pens have a natural tendency to disappear into thin air after you have used them for a few minutes.'

At least, that's what I think he said, on account of the fact that I was using the sharp end of a peacock feather dipped in cold tea to take notes at the time. This despite checking that I had a pen on me before leaving home to do the interview.

It was a Maruzen felt-tip, No. 37P, with gold-and-black stripes and 'Japan' written in sort-of Italic letters on the casing. I know, because I took it out of my shirt pocket to make sure it still had some ink in the barrel before I put it behind my ear when the phone rang while I was looking for a piece of paper to test it out on. I think.

Or did I leave it in the shirt that I had to throw in the washing because the dog leaped up on me as I tried to remember where I put my car-keys before leaving the house? I'm not sure now. But I know it was there sometime this morning.

Would the person who finds it please forward it to me as soon as possible, and in return I will send a personally written note of utmost gratitude. Well, as soon as I can find my pen. Thanks.

THE TROUBLE WITH AEROBICS

Aerobics and aerobatics. I always get confused. Which is the one where you fly upside-down in a small aeroplane, until the blood starts rushing to your head and you feel a hollow, pounding sensation in the pit of your stomach? Oh. Right.

So aerobics must be the one where you put on a leotard and jump up and down until the blood starts rushing to your head and you feel a hollow, pounding sensation in the pit of your stomach. I thought so.

It's just that I keep forgetting, because the human mind has an amazing capacity for erasing every memory of the unspeakable agony that shoots through your system when you are engaged in a session of aerobics.

The throbbing vascular migraine, the dizziness, the shortness of breath, the uncontrollable feeling of incipient nausea . . . let me tell you, ladies and gentlemen, it's terrible. And I'm not even talking about the exercises. I'm talking about the music.

Tina Turner singing 'You're the best, better than all the rest'. Donna Summer singing 'Ooh, love to love you, baby'. Frankie Goes to Hollywood singing 'Relax, don't do it, when you want to sock it to it'. Right Said Fred singing 'I'm too sexy for my shorts'.

Now don't get me wrong. I have nothing in principle against music of this nature, as long as it is experienced within its proper cultural context, which is as far away from me as possible. Indeed, it is only because I couldn't stand the music that I recently decided to stop going to aerobics classes in someone's garage every Monday, Tuesday, and Thursday evening between 6 pm and 7 pm.

The most beneficial aerobic exercise of them all — switching off the music

I mean, everything else about aerobics classes I really like: the full-length mirrors on the wall, the rhythmic stomp of takkies on floorboards, the discreetly perspiring ladies in their leotards and leggings, the exercises... well, some of the exercises.

In particular, I'm thinking about 'the cool-down', which is the exercise you do when the clock on the wall says two minutes to seven, and you can finally take your eyes off the clock on the wall. The aerobics teacher says, 'OK, everyone, it's time for the cool-down', and you lie in the dark with your eyes closed, feeling warm waves of relaxation wash over every muscle in your body.

You breathe in. You breathe out. You clench your fists. You unclench your fists. You think of nothing. You go home. I have always found this exercise to be very beneficial to the circulation, and no matter how busy I may be during the course of the day, I always set aside a few hours to lie in the dark and think of nothing.

Sometimes I might vary the exercise by lying on the couch and watching television while thinking of nothing, and other times I might perform the exercise in a seated position during an important business meeting. Either way, unlike many people in today's fast-moving, stress-filled society, I firmly believe that a little aerobic exercise never hurt anybody, which is why I try and do as little aerobic exercise as possible.

I mean, just look what it did to Jane Fonda. Before she invented aerobics in 1982, Fonda was an award-winning actress who single-handedly changed the course of the Vietnam War. But today, she is known only for being married to Ted Turner and single-handedly changing the course of the American Presidency. (She voted for Hilary.)

If it wasn't for all those stupid aerobic workout tapes and videos, Jane Fonda would probably be President herself. OK, she'd also be 25 kg heavier around the hips, and about $10-billion lighter around the wallet.

But my point is, what good is a fantastic figure and heaps of money, when you have to do 25 abdominal lifts, 50 sit-ups, 40 knee-and-thigh stretches and 20 hamstring pulls every morning before you even begin your main aerobic exercise session of the day?

Hey, I'm not saying you shouldn't exercise. I'm just saying there must be better ways, not to mention better music. For instance, if you really want to 'work out', if you really want to 'feel the burn', if you really want to 'trim body fat by up to 25 per cent', why not follow my personal exercise routine, which I call 'Avoiding Exercise'.

Here's what you do:

(1) Wake up at 6 am on the dot.
(2) Stre-e-e-e-e-tch across the bedside table for the television remote control.
(3) Switch on TV.
(4) Watch 'Body Beat'.
(5) Switch off TV.
(6) Stre-e-e-e-e-tch out across bed.
(7) Go back to sleep.
(8) Wake up at 8.30 am on the dot and realise with a panic that you are supposed to be at work at 7.15 am.
(9) Do one sit-up.
(10) Go out to work.
(11) Get fired.
(12) Feel the burn.
(13) Trim body fat by up to 25 per cent.
(14) Take up aerobatics.

Hey, you know what they say. No pain, no gain. Which one are we talking about again?

MAGNUM FARCE

There was a time, not so long ago, when the most embarrassing thing a guy could do was walk into a chemist and try to buy a condom. But those days of shame and innocence are over now, and the only remaining embarrassment lies in the field of personal protection. Firearms.

The question, of course, is not whether you should buy yourself one. The question is how. On the surface, it seems a simple enough proposition. You walk into a gunshop, point at a gun, and walk out with a loaded weapon in your pocket. But it's not that easy.

For one thing, you don't just walk into gunshops. Unlike chemists, these establishments do not automatically open their doors to casual browsers. They've got security. Barred, double-bolted, wired to the buzzer behind the counter, the gates of a gunshop open only for the serious browser.

You stand at the threshold, wondering why they need all this security when they've got all those guns, and the guy in the flak-jacket looks you over. You begin to feel like one of those silhouettes hanging on the wall, with a bull's-eye in the region of your heart. (Five points. Two points for an ear.) The guy in the flak-jacket decides you're probably not carrying a gun, and even if you were, you wouldn't know how to use it. He's right.

Bzzzt. The gate swings open. Clang. The gate swings shut. You take a look around. It's quiet. You're in the sanctuary of wholesale violence, retail division. Giant posters of golden-

'Er . . . on second thoughts, I'll just take this toothpick for my
Swiss knife, thanks.'

bodied, lead-headed bullets on the wall. Fishing knives, crossbows, an antelope with its antlers framed in the cross-hairs of a telescopic sight. Great: if an elk ever breaks into your home at two in the morning, you'll know exactly what to do. Right now, you're just browsing. Seriously.

There are guns, pistols, revolvers all over the place, and you don't know how you're going to admit that you can't tell the difference. You're going to have to play it safe and talk about 'firearms'. But what's the problem? You know about these things. You've seen the movies.

You know that Dirty Harry carries a Smith & Wesson .44 Magnum, Model 29, sometimes referred to as a 'day-maker'. You know that James Bond uses a Walther PPK 9mm combat pistol, but only when he really has to. Trouble is, you're not Dirty Harry. You're not James Bond. You're just an everyday South African citizen, out to make an everyday South African purchase.

'Can I help you?' You're studying the range, the guns, the pistols, the revolvers, neatly nestled under glass with tags attached to their triggers, like exhibits in a courtroom. The prices seem a bit steep. Two and a half grand for a gun? And it doesn't look like a Magnum, either. 'Yes. I . . . I'm looking for . . . do you stock those little plastic toothpicks for Swiss Knives?'

OK. You've got your plastic toothpick (R2,50, excluding tax). But while you're here, you may as well tap the glass. Just an impulse. 'I'm also interested in a . . . firearm. Something small, for home security purposes.' Flak-jacket looks you straight in the eyes. He doesn't believe a word of it. He could tell as soon as you walked in the door. You're looking for something big. To rob a bank. No. To rob a gunshop.

'Pistol or revolver?' Your heart's beating so fast now, a guy could probably aim a gun at you and get five points in the dark. 'Well, I'm not sure...what would you recommend?' You can feel Flak-jacket's fists tighten. This is the dumbest question he's ever heard. What is he, a wine steward? He folds his arms and fires an even dumber question. 'Are you looking for something to carry on your person?'

You laugh nervously. What a crazy idea! You were hoping they'd deliver to your home. 'No, not to carry. It would just be something to use around the house.' Flak-jacket taps the glass. 'Pistol.' You're starting to sweat. You want to run out of here and never walk into a gunshop again. But two things stand in your way. The gate's locked. And you haven't paid for the toothpick.

'Pistol. I see. Tell me, are they ... easier to handle?' Flak-jacket reaches under the glass and pulls out a pistol. It's not loaded. Of course. You knew that. 'I'd say their main advantage is that they're lighter than a revolver, and they're easier to carry on your person.' Suddenly, you've got a pistol in your hands. It's a Z88 9mm Parabellum, made in South Africa. R2 500.

The last time you held a firearm, you were in the Army. That was an R-1 rifle. You called it a gun. Result: 150 push-ups. When you pulled the trigger, you didn't only miss the target, you missed the sandbank behind the target. But this is different. This is smooth, comfortable, easy to handle. Like a black mamba.

A purely hypothetical question. 'Say I was to buy this gun. How soon could I get it?' A purely hypothetical answer. 'You put down a deposit, and we send off your application for a licence. Probably take between three and six weeks. Then you get your firearm.'

You slide the Z88 9mm Parabellum across the glass counter. You'll think about it. You pay for the toothpick, and the door clangs shut behind you. Three to six weeks! You feel a little better. It's not as easy as you thought it was for any idiot off the street to buy a firearm. But what about you? You're a reasonable, responsible, law-abiding citizen. Why should you feel like a criminal, just because you're trying to buy a gun? OK. Forget it. Just one question. Anybody know where a guy can get hold of a good flak-jacket?

HOOT IF YOU LOVE BUMPER-STICKERS

Everywhere I go these days, on the highways, byways, freeways and toll-ways of our nation, I keep bumping into people who are driven by an overwhelming urge to tell me that they are committed to peace, that they are only visiting this planet, and that they will smash-a my face if I touch-a their car.

Stuck behind them in bumper-to-bumper traffic, I read the writing on their rear-ends with a certain wry detachment, because I know that they are really trying to tell me only one thing. 'This is my car, and it's in front of you.'

Since the primary purpose of driving on South African roads is to get in front of other cars, and the secondary purpose is to prevent other cars from getting in front of you, it follows that bumper-stickers are the most popular and effective means of driver-to-driver communication, next to rolling down the window and making signals with your fist.

As the sort of motorist who is always being overtaken by other motorists, despite the fact that I keep well within the speed-limit while travelling in the fast lane, I have had plenty of opportunity to study bumper-stickers at close quarters, and my conclusion is that they have a very positive role to play in encouraging safe driving habits.

For instance, if I see a car up ahead with a sticker on its bumper, I am immediately compelled to maintain a following distance of between one and two metres, as opposed to the average South African following distance of 2,5 cm.

The reason is that when you are too close to someone's bumper, the stickers are often obscured by the angle of your bonnet and the intensity of the other person's exhaust emissions, making it almost impossible to decipher such messages as 'Get off my back', 'If you can read this, you are too darn close', and — Screech! Tinkle! Crunch! — 'This taxi stops anywhere, anytime, anyplace'.

But the really big advantage of bumper-stickers, from a safety point of view, is that they can be used to cover up unsightly bumps and dents caused by people slamming into you from behind when you change your mind about overtaking someone at the last minute because you haven't finished reading their bumper-stickers yet.

After all, bumper-stickers are among the few things you are legally allowed to read while driving, the others being advertising billboards, political campaign posters, and War and Peace by Leo Tolstoy, albeit only in the southbound lane of the M1 freeway at 7.55 am on a Monday morning.

As a regular reader of bumper-stickers — sometimes, when there is nothing on TV and I have finished reading the sides of every cornflake packet in the house, I will even get in my car and cruise around the hypermarket in the hope of spotting a few bumpers I haven't read yet — I believe that the modern bumper-sticker can be divided into three basic categories.

The first is Unsolicited Testimonials, such as 'I Love Radio 5', or 'Mario's Panel-Beaters — We Fix Bumpers'. These stickers, often attached to bumpers without the prior knowledge or approval of the bumpee, are regarded with scorn by true bumper-sticker aficionados, since their sole purpose is to save giant corporations the trouble and expense of distributing advertising and promotional material themselves.

On the other hand, since it is sometimes possible to win up to R250 in cash prizes if your Unsolicited Testimonial is spotted by an eagle-eyed marketing executive or disc-jockey, there is probably no harm in affixing a few such stickers all over your bumper and hooting to draw attention to yourself as you drive up and down the street outside the company's head office.

This brings us to the second category of bumper-sticker, which is Existential Philosophy. Here we find such gems of other people's thoughts as 'Born to Shop', 'I Think, Therefore I Am . . . I Think', 'Just Because I'm Paranoid Doesn't Mean You're Not Following Me', and 'Why Be Normal', normally stuck upside-down and in mirror-writing on the front bumper.

Loaded with pithy wit and the wisdom of the sages, stickers of this type mark the driver as a person of great taste and intellectual vitality, who just happens to be driving someone else's car while his is in the garage.

Our third category is the Territorial Imperative bumper-sticker, as epitomised by 'As A Matter of Fact, I Do Own the Road', 'If You Don't Like the Way I Drive, Stay Off the

Pavement', and 'Warning — This Pantechnicon Has 32 Wheels and Goes On Forever'.

Then we have the fourth category, which is — did I say there were only three categories? OK, so I made a mistake! — Non-Verbal bumper-stickers, among them the Splat of Paint, the Fake Bullet-Hole, and Bart Simpson Making a Rude Sign. The growing popularity of these stickers is a sure sign of the pervasive influence of the visual media in today's society, as well as rapidly declining attention spans among the... where was I again?

Oh, yes. The fifth category: Bumper-Stickers About Sex. The sixth category: Bumper-Stickers About Golf. The seventh category: Bumper-Stickers That Prove You Have Been to the Kruger National Park or the Blyde River Canyon. The eighth category: Fish. OK, that's enough categories.

The point is, bumper-stickers represent a wide field of interest not only for students of sociology and contemporary automotive culture, but for serious collectors who would like to get involved in this rewarding and fascinating hobby. If you are serious about becoming a collector of bumper-stickers, there are really only two things you have to remember.

One: always make sure that your chisel is sharp. Two: make sure that you don't get caught by the owner of the car as he returns from his shopping. Otherwise, like the bumper-sticker says, he smash-a your face.

YOU'VE COME A LONG WAY, BABY

Until the other day, if you had to ask me what a 'Caesar' was, I would have told you it's a kind of salad you get with your pizza in an Italian restaurant. Well, I still think that's what it is, although, to be quite frank, I usually order a Greek.

But the point is, I now know that a 'Caesar' is also something else altogether. It's one of the two main ways ladies have babies. Ask me. I was there.

'Will you be coming to theatre?' asked the anaesthetist, or was it the anaesthesiologist, as he gave my wife an epidural, or was it a giant needle in her back? My gut reaction was the same as it always is when people ask me whether I would like to go to the theatre, namely, 'No thanks, I'd rather stay home and watch a video.'

But the guy assured me that the whole performance would be over in 20 minutes, max, and that I would be home in time to miss the traffic. That's the nice thing about Caesars, or 'Caesarean Sections', as us experts sometimes call them.

Because of the way they are done — surgeon makes incision in abdomen, whips baby out, zips lady back together again — Caesareans can be scheduled for any time of day that is convenient for doctor and patient. This is not the case with 'labour', which usually takes place at the most inconvenient hour of day or night, such as when doctor is about to tee off at 18th hole or husband is sitting at home trying to watch a video.

As someone who goes out of his way to avoid labour, I can understand why more and more modern women are choosing to have Caesarean Sections. Indeed, more Caesareans are performed in South Africa than in any other country in the Western world, according to a statistic I just made up, so it was no real surprise when the doctor said: 'Be at the clinic at 2.30 pm. And bring your wife.'

Oh, I forgot to tell you what an epidural is. It's a kind of injection that sends half of you to sleep, while the other half stays awake and has a conversation with your husband. 'Stop reading that newspaper,' said my wife. 'Are you crazy? And put that Coke down! You can't drink in here! Did you remember to feed the cats?'

This was in a sort of pre-theatre 'holding bay', where they leave you alone after the epidural to spend some quality time with your husband. But I had hardly finished reading the Sports Pages when a nurse barged through the swing-doors and said: 'All right, who's having the Caesar? Come on, we haven't got all day!'

Well, something like that. In any case, before I knew it, my wife was taking the trolley to theatre, while I was standing in the changing-room, putting on green drawstring trousers, a green sleeveless shirt, a blue hairnet, blue covers for my shoes, and a surgical mask.

I must admit, at this point, I was feeling a little nervous. Somehow, I had always thought that the doctor was going to be doing the Caesar.

So I was relieved to find, upon entering the theatre, that all I actually had to do was sit on a small chair and hold my wife's hand in case I fainted. I looked around the room. Bright yellow lights blazed overhead, while monitors blipped, oxygen hissed, and instruments clattered on a tray. Everyone wore green. It was 3 pm. A scalpel descended.

I have always been in awe of medical men. They are so good at telling jokes. 'Winnie Mandela moves in next door to Eugene Terre'Blanche,' said the doctor, his scalpel slicing through layers of flesh and tissue like a hot knife through butter. Well, I'm guessing here.

Congratulations! It's a Caesar

Some things you just don't want to see, such as your wife's internal organs and any movie starring Christopher Lambert. I looked at the lights instead. My wife asked me if I was feeling OK.

The senior assistant nurse handed the doctor a wad of swabs, and he said: 'So one day, Winnie goes over to introduce herself, right? Because she doesn't want Eugene to think she's being unfriendly. And they get on so well, like a house on fire, that Eugene insists on giving Winnie a present. A little dog. Oh, she says, what's his name? And Eugene says: "His name is Canteen."'

One thing I never realised about surgical lights before. They're reflective. The more you look at them to avoid looking at what's happening down below, the more they give you a crystal-clear reflection of what's happening down below. So I watched. Hey, some guys bring video cameras.

The doctor finished his joke. It had my wife in stitches for a week. I'd like to tell you the punchline, honest I would, but all I can remember is: 3,08 kg, 48 cm, 3.37 pm. Girl. I know. I was there, and I wouldn't have missed it for anything in the world. Well, except maybe one of those nice salads you get with your pizza in an Italian restaurant. What are they called again?

JUNK FOOD FOR THOUGHT

According to the side of a packet of cornflakes I was reading over breakfast the other day, it has become more important than ever for people in today's fast-paced society to maintain a healthy lifestyle by following a nutritionally balanced diet.

The secret of a truly balanced diet — pizza on one knee and beermug on the other

What this means, in practice, is that if you begin your day with a bowl of high-fibre oat-bran cereal, a spoonful of low-fat yoghurt, a glass of boiled water with lemon juice, and a thin slice of unbuttered wholewheat toast, you should be sure to balance it later in the day with something wholesome and nutritious, such as food.

By this I mean anything that falls into one of the four basic food groups, which are: Chocolate; Pizza; Potato Chips; and Beer. Taken alone or together, these foods have been found to satisfy up to 65 per cent of the RDA (Recommended Daily Allowance) of proteins, carbohydrates, vitamins, zinc, iron, riboflavin, and federally approved preservatives, with the remaining 35 per cent coming from more chocolate, pizza, potato chips, and beer.

But even the most carefully balanced diet, for instance, a box of pizza on your knee and a bottle of Castle Lager on the arm of the sofa, will be of no lasting benefit if it is not accompanied by a scientifically formulated exercise programme. It is therefore strongly advised that you get up every now and again to change the channel yourself.

Remember, the primary function of food is to supply the body with the energy it needs to get in the car and drive to the shop to pick up the video, so either ask them to deliver it to you, or start right away on the following proven regime of 'healthy eating habits for people in today's fast-paced society'.

Rule Number One is 'Don't Eat Between Snacks', unless you are hungry, bored, under stress, depressed, or standing next to the buffet table at a cocktail party while someone is making a speech. The second rule is 'Stop Putting So Much Salt On Your Food'.

Nutritionists and my wife point out that an excess of salt in one's diet is a leading cause of hypertension, second only to trying to get some salt out of a cellar by sticking the prong of a fork in the holes. Healthy eating tip: don't bother! Just use a few of those little sachets that you get on the airplane instead.

Then we come to one of the mainstays of healthy eating, which is 'No Dressing On Salads'. Dressing, for example French, Italian, Thousand Island, or Waldorf, is known to be one of the primary causes of high cholesterol in salad, and should therefore be strictly avoided by the health-conscious diner. However, since dressing is also the primary cause of taste in salad, my suggestion would be that you go one step further and avoid the salad altogether, making up for it with an extra helping of ice-cream and hot chocolate sauce.

This brings us on to fibre, an important aspect of anyone's diet. Fibre is commonly found in porridge, barley, gem-squash, seaweed, and string, and its chief benefit, aside from the fact that it helps to take your mind off food, is that it 'keeps you regular'. My advice: get a watch.

We will now briefly investigate the area of food preparation. After all, it's not just what you eat, it's what happened to it before it got on to your plate. Was it boiled? Grilled? Battered? Thawed? Microwaved? Barbecued? Poached? Rotisseried? Good. As long as it wasn't fried. Experts and my wife agree that frying is one of the major health hazards related to eating, as well as being a leading cause of fires in the kitchen. So don't fry anything. Ask your wife to do it.

This leaves us only with the thorny issue of 'Vegetarianism'. Is it OK, people often ask me, to include fish, meat, and poultry in one's diet? My answer is yes, as long as you have enough room on your plate. But I would qualify this by saying that you should avoid ordering or eating anything that in any way resembles whatever it was before it became food.

Food? Did somebody mention food? It's been at least 20 minutes since I popped into the kitchen for a handful of kettle-fried crisps and a stick of kudu biltong, so if you'll excuse me, I'm going to stop talking about food while I go and balance my diet. After all, you are what you eat. So who wants to be an oat-bran flake?

I LOVE MY BANK

When people who live in such boring countries as New Zealand or Antarctica ask me to name one good reason why I continue to stay in South Africa, I always puff out my chest and say: 'Well, for one thing, South Africa has the highest per capita rate of automatic bank-teller machines anywhere in the Western world.'

This is a fact I gleaned from an authoritative advertising supplement on trends in electronic banking, and although I have slight reservations about the 'per capita' and 'Western world' parts of the statement, I have no reason to doubt that it is fundamentally true.

After all, I have visited several countries in the Western world, and I have yet to come across a single auto-teller that can do withdrawals, deposits, inter-account transfers and mini-statement enquiries on any of my six South African auto-teller cards.

At home, on the other hand, there is a gleaming, state-of-the-art auto-teller on every street corner, and all I have to do is insert my card and punch in my PIN number to be granted instant access to the full range of electronic banking facilities.

Indeed, I hardly ever go into a bank these days, unless it is to tell the lady behind the Enquiries counter that the auto-teller has swallowed my card. Even when this does happen, it is usually for a very good reason, such as the fact that the machine is currently in an 'off-line' mode of operation due to having swallowed too many cards.

In any case, there can be no denying that auto-tellers save time, money, aggravation, and the enormous amount of energy and self-confidence required to look an actual human being in the eye and say 'good morning'. My philosophy here is simple.

Why go inside and be held up in a bank queue for hours, when you can stand outside and be mugged in an auto-teller queue for no extra charge? That's what I call customer care and convenience. But my real point is, banks and bankers just don't get the credit they deserve from the South African public.

Everywhere you go, you hear people complaining. If they're not complaining about the rising overdraft rate, they're complaining about the plummeting interest rate. If they're not complaining about rude, inefficient bank tellers, they're complaining about rude, inefficient bank managers.

If they're not complaining about the fact that you can't find a deposit or withdrawal slip anywhere in the banking hall, they're complaining about the fact that they've been stuck for 20 minutes inside the bullet-proof plate-glass security cubicle that is supposed to open up when the little green light comes on. Well, I am here to tell you that I don't have any complaints.

The longest I have ever had to wait in the security cubicle was ten minutes, and, now that I think of it, I can't recall having had to wait longer than double that for a deposit or withdrawal slip from the lady at Enquiries. But the main thing is, I have always been very pleased with the level of customer service at my bank.

For instance, I recently discovered that a stop-order from my current account had not been paid into my bond account for the third month in a row. When I enquired about this, I was given a full and satisfactory explanation within minutes. 'I'm sorry, the computer lost it.'

In so many so-called service industries today, people are quick to put the blame for a problem or mistake on one of their fellow-workers. But in all my years of banking at my bank, not once have I encountered a person who has made a mistake. Oh, hang on a second, I have. Me.

Let's see. That makes four cheques that have been returned to my current account this month on the grounds that 'client's signature is different'. That's true. I have noticed that my signature is different to other clients' signatures. So I can't complain about that.

But what about last week, when I was checking out of the Umtata Holiday Inn, and the guy behind the desk told me that there was a 'Hold and Call' on my credit card?

As everyone knows, this means the card has been reported as stolen, and the person attempting to pass it off as his own should be held until the police arrive. Fortunately, on this occasion, they did not arrive, as it was an early check-out.

I must admit, when I telephoned the Customer Relations Department of my bank to find out why I had been reported as having stolen my own credit card, I was immediately put through to the first available Customer Relations Assistant after five minutes of listening to the cellophane-and-comb version of Für Elise by Ludwig Van Beethoven.

Then I heard the sound of a computer keyboard tapping as the lady erased the 'Hold and Call' on my credit card, and I was given a crisp, clear, and concise explanation of the circumstances surrounding the incident. 'I'm sorry, Sir, I have absolutely no idea.'

That's what I like about banks. If only we could get that ruthless efficiency and striving for service excellence transferred to other areas of South African industry, such as airline reservations offices. Until then, I can't think of a better reason for staying in the country.

HOW TO BLUFF YOUR WAY THROUGH AN ART MOVIE

The artist Andy Warhol, fleetingly famous for declaring that everyone in the world would one day be famous for 15 minutes, once made a movie about a day in the life of the Empire State Building in New York.

The word 'movie' is used advisedly here, since Andy Warhol's Empire consisted of a single static shot of the Empire State Building doing what skyscrapers do best, that is to say, just standing there being a monolith.

Nothing wrong with that — after all, Charles Bronson's acting style is based on the same principle — except that the film lasted about 11 and three quarter hours longer than 15 minutes.

By contrast, Andy Warhol's Sleep runs for a mere six hours, and consists of a single static shot of a man in the process of being fast asleep, presumably during a screening of Andy Warhol's Empire. A critic of the time says Andy Warhol's Sleep is a movie 'not so much to be watched, as experienced', and although I cannot claim to have had the experience, I can claim to have slept through enough Art Movies to call myself an expert on the subject.

So what can I tell you? Perhaps I can begin with a broad definition of an Art Movie, which is 'any foreign-language picture which runs for a maximum of two days in a 20-seat movie theatre in the Northern Suburbs, and which does not star Arnold Schwarzenegger as a robot from the future'.

I will briefly discuss the sole exception to this rule, which is when the movie is in English and you are watching it in a foreign country. I once attended a screening of Rambo 2 in Tel Aviv, and while Sylvester Stallone spoke fluent American throughout, the Hebrew and Arabic subtitles were large enough to obscure all of his major muscle groupings, except for the tricep in his left nostril during the famous '15 Communists with one head-butt' sequence. This made it an Art Movie.

Generally, however, conflict in Art Movies is of an internal rather than external nature, a fine example being the scene in which Liv Ullman fights with her mother during Ingmar Bergman's masterpiece of the Swedish Cinema, Autumn Sonata.

As you may recall, unless you were asleep at the time, Liv Ullman plays the estranged daughter of a famous concert pianist who is always too busy playing the piano to talk to her daughter. Much of the movie consists of Liv Ullman and her mother not talking to each other, and after one particularly gruelling exchange of sidelong glances, Liv begins to get really irritated with the situation.

Now, if this had been a normal movie, Liv would have picked up a large blunt object, such as a television set, and hurled it through the diningroom window while screaming 'I'm mad as hell and I'm not going to take it any more' in Swedish.

But because this is an Art Movie, all she does is fix her withering gaze on a point 15 cm beyond the cameraman's left ear, while her mother, played by Ingrid Bergman, stands in the background and fixes her withering gaze on Liv Ullman. This brings us to the first and most important rule of Art Movie-watching, which is 'NEVER CONFUSE INGMAR BERGMAN, THE SWEDISH DIRECTOR, WITH INGRID BERGMAN, THE ACTRESS'.

It is a very easy mistake to make, and often the only way to tell the difference is to wake up during an Ingmar Bergman movie and look at the screen to see if Ingrid Bergman is acting in it. Remember, Ingmar is the director, and directors are always the most important people associated with the making of an Art Movie, which is why their names always come before the movie in any group discussion on the subject.

Hence: 'What would you prefer to see tonight, darling? Ingmar Bergman's Persona (1966), or Jean-Luc Godard's Nouvelle Vague (1990)? How about Akira Kurosawa's Yojimbo (1961), or Francois Truffaut's Jules et Jim (1961)? Or perhaps you would prefer Federico Fellini's Otto e Mezzo (1963)? Hmmm?'

'Hmmm, darling, that really is a tough choice. Why don't we rather hire an Arnold Schwarzenegger movie and pick up a couple of takeaways from Luigi's Pizza Parlour (1992) along the way?'

This brings us to the second important rule of Art Movie-watching, which is 'NEVER ATTEMPT TO WATCH AN ART MOVIE WHILE EATING A TAKEAWAY PIZZA'. The reason is that, according to a recent scientific experiment involving a Margherita With Green Peppers and a rental copy of Bernardo Bertolucci's 311-minute masterpiece of the Italian Cinema, 1900 (1977), it is quite difficult to concentrate on the subtitles on a television screen while you are trying to eat a piece of Italian food.

In fact, I would go so far as to say that you should not attempt to watch an Art Movie on television under any circumstances at all. Rather, you should go to an Art Movie theatre, where you will be able to demonstrate to the other two people in the audience that you are the sort of person who demands more from a motion picture than Sylvester Stallone head-butting 15 Communists at once.

This brings us to the third rule of Art Movie-watching, which is 'NEVER READ THE SUBTITLES ALOUD TO YOURSELF DURING THE SCREENING OF AN ART MOVIE IN A BONA FIDE ART MOVIE ESTABLISHMENT'. The reason for this is that you might wake the other two people up.

If you have difficulty following the subtitles from a distance of more than 3 metres, try and get a seat in the middle of the front row. Not only will you be able to read the subtitles with ease, but the movie will also appear grainy and distorted, and you will not be able to make any sense of the plot at all. That's why they call it an Art Movie. Goodnight, and enjoy the show.

HOW TO DRIVE YOURSELF CRAZY

Before setting off on any journey of more than a few hundred kilometres across the rugged, ever-changing landscape of our nation, I always take a couple of minutes to make sure that my motorcar is in tip-top condition.

I check the indicators, left and right. I pump the brake-pedal and crank up the handbrake. I flick the lights on to bright, watch the petrol-gauge rise from Empty to Full, and test the windscreen-wipers on slow, intermittent, and fast. I ease the clutch in and out, put my foot down on the accelerator, and press my palm against the hooter for one or two seconds.

Then, when I am a hundred per cent satisfied that all systems are go, I step outside, lock the doors, arm the immobiliser, and hurry across the parking-lot to check in for my flight. Hey, I'm not crazy. I'm not going to drive when I can fly.

I'm going to sit here in my window seat, swizzling the ice in my ginger-ale as I throw back another fistful of salted peanuts, for it is only up here in the clouds that one is able to maintain the necessary perspective on the mechanics of long-distance motoring. In my experience, it is the rule of the road. The further you travel, the sooner you are going to have to call a mechanic.

I mean, look at that guy down there with acrid plumes of black smoke pouring out from underneath his bonnet. Or how about that guy, just a fingernail further along, with a puncture in his right front tyre. (I'm just guessing here. From this distance, it could just as easily be a ruptured sump.)

Or that guy — OK, could be a woman — with bonnet and boot-lid yawning in the universal signal for: 'Help. My car won't go. Don't ask me why. It was going fine when I left home this morning. Then I turned on to the freeway and it started spluttering and making funny noises. But don't worry. I've got my bonnet and my boot-lid up, and I'll get it going again as soon as I can work out where the engine is.'

I know the feeling. I've been there. At least, I would have been there if my car hadn't started spluttering and making funny noises as soon as I turned on to the freeway. Fortunately, I was only going as far as the airport, so I was able to thumb a lift from a passing pick-up truck, but my big question is, why do these things happen?

Why are today's motorcars so afraid of the freeway, that they begin abdicating their very function at the first sighting of a big blue roadsign riddled with bullet-holes? Come to think of it, why do people have to shoot at roadsigns, anyway?

In my experience, if you're going to get bored on a long journey, there is nothing like a good book and a game of Scrabble to while away the hours between the first signs of total engine-failure and the first heart-stopping appearance of the emergency mechanic in the shimmering heat haze on the horizon.

But that's beside the point. The point is, you hardly ever see a car broken down on its way to the video-shop around the corner, or the after-hours chemist across the road.

Even the most reliable car I ever owned, a 1973 Alfa Romeo Guilietta that could be relied upon to stop going as soon as it saw its first stop-sign of the day, had no trouble making it to any service station that happened to be located on a downhill. But in the long run — forget it. Total engine failure.

No sooner have the school-bells pealed for the start of the holidays, or the factories locked their doors for another

Why nine out of ten motorists prefer flying.
(The tenth prefers walking)

official or unofficial long weekend, than the verges of our national highways are crammed with the carcasses of cars that were going fine when they left home this morning.

I have thought long and hard about this phenomenon, and I believe I have come up with the answer. The answer is 'human error'. Yes, it is sad but true: people don't make cars like they used to.

I was speaking to my mechanic about this, the last time he charged me R750 (excluding VAT) for replacing the oil seal on my radiator, or was it the bearing on my sump? Anyway, he was saying that cars these days are specifically designed to 'conk in' within two and a half hours or 50 km of your front gate, whichever comes first. I had to agree with him.

Only a couple of months ago, I was forced to pull on to the shoulder of the R544 to Potgietersrus, when all four red lights on my instrument panel began flashing at once. At first I thought it was just a short-circuit caused by excessive bass on the cassette-machine, which was playing the bit where the cannons go crazy on Tschaikovsky's 1812 Overture.

Then plumes of yellow smoke, accompanied by a fine spray of boiling water, began oozing out of the apertures of my car, and my average speed suddenly dropped to 15 km/h in the fast lane. Then, for no reason at all, 220 km from Potgietersrus, my car stopped going altogether.

I was later told that this was due to 'overheating in empty radiator' (R1 200 excluding VAT), yet I distinctly remember filling up the little plastic windscreen-washer thing with water before leaving home that morning. Which just goes to show.

Or how about that time, 42 km from Nababeep on the R542, when my engine kept 'cutting out', apparently because of a 'faulty alternator' (R1 750 excluding VAT)?

My big question is, if an alternator develops a fault, what happens to the thing with which it is supposed to alternate? They can't both be faulty at the same time, can they?

As far as I'm concerned, it is all part of the rapid breakdown in standards of motorcar design and manufacture, and I, for one, have had enough. Enough of bald tyres. Blocked fuel pumps. Dirty spark-plugs. Clogged pistons. Blown gaskets. Dry battery-wells. Universal joints that mysteriously fall off when you go over a speed-bump at 90 km/h.

It's enough to drive you crazy, if only for short distances at a time. Hey, anyone know of a good emergency mechanic who can give me a lift home from the airport?

HEY, HEY, ROCK 'N ROLL!

In any list of the Ten Greatest Movies Ever Made, right up there with Citizen Kane and Lawrence of Arabia, you're probably not going to find Rob Reiner's Spinal Tap. But that's only because it's in a category and genre all of its own: the mock rock documentary, or, if you will, 'rockumentary'.

On the face of it, and even on the bottom, the movie is a straightforward chronicle of a disastrous American tour by a three-piece English rock band who are long past their sell-by date. Once in the major league of Heavy Metal heroes, the fictitious but uncannily authentic Spinal Tap now find themselves rocking on their laurels in a desperate bid to re-ignite the spontaneous combustion of their power-and-glory days. But things, as we soon discover, go wrong. Horribly wrong.

Gigs are cancelled through lack of interest, 'technical difficulties' befuddle their stage shows, and the festering acrimony of life on the road drives a wedge between the, um, artists and their management. For this is a band so devoid of artistic direction, that they can't even find their way from the dressing-room to the front of the stage.

We see them fumbling their way down a labyrinth of corridors, bumping into each other as the roar of the thinned-out crowd grows louder in the distance, not with adulation, but impatience. Finally, they burst on to a stage shrouded in a swirling green mist, which parts to reveal the band members locked inside giant plexiglass seed-pods.

To the cue of a thunderous guitar-riff, the pods burst open, and the band bloom into ear-splitting action. Except for the bass guitarist. Trapped inside his pod by a minor technical malfunction, he pummels away in silent panic for a few minutes, hoping to attract someone's attention before his oxygen runs out.

It is moments like this that make Rob Reiner's Spinal Tap such a glorious parody of the attitudes, platitudes, and pretensions of the rock 'n roll biz, and although the director has gone on to Hollywood mainstream fame with such mega-hits as A Few Good Men and When Harry Met Sally, he has never made anything quite as perceptive or hysterically funny.

Although the movie sank without trace on circuit, it has since become a cult favourite of rock 'n roll fans and bands alike. Indeed, once you have seen Spinal Tap a few times, it is impossible to sit through a real live concert by a real live rock band without being overwhelmed by the uncanny feeling that life, once again, is imitating art. Example: Foreigner.

The American rock band, a hit-machine of the mid-Seventies and Eighties, recently toured South Africa for the first time in their history and ours. Like Spinal Tap, Foreigner have seen and heard better days, but it is the memory of those better days that fuels them and acts as a magnet for their fans across the globe. Those who are less convinced about Foreigner's relevance in the Nineties might be tempted to dismiss the band as 'dinosaurs', but it is worth pointing out that in the Nineties, dinosaurs are very big indeed.

And so it was no surprise to see the Standard Bank Arena packed to sweating, stomping, swaying capacity when Foreigner kicked off their nationwide tour in Johannesburg. Nor was it a surprise to see anything else that Foreigner and their fans did that evening.

A good rock 'n roll concert is a conspiracy of clichés between an act and its audience, and it is with this in mind, as a student of Spinal Tap and a closet fan of Foreigner, that I have identified the following Ten Greatest Rock 'n Roll Concert Clichés of All Time. Whether the venue is Tokyo or Johannesburg, whether the act is Spinal Tap or Foreigner, no concert is complete without them.

(1)   Late Starts. Ideally, the show should get underway no sooner than 45 minutes after the advertised kick-off time. This gives the fans an opportunity to work themselves into a frenzy of Mexican waves and slow hand-claps, while the band attempt to find their way from the dressing-room to the stage.

(2)   False Starts. Suddenly, someone in the audience notices that a man in jeans and black T-shirt is fiddling with a guitar, or clicking his tongue at a microphone. A lone cheer rises from the auditorium, until the person in question realises he has been watching a member of the technical crew testing the equipment.

(3) 'Hello, wherever we are!' At last, the show begins with a plunge into darkness, an explosion of pyrotechnics, and a song nobody recognises because of the ringing in their ears. Then the spotlight falls on the slightly paunchy, slightly balding lead singer, who pauses to catch his breath before greeting the city by name. In Spinal Tap, it was 'Hello, Cleveland!', even when the band were playing Chicago; at the Foreigner concert, it was 'Hello, Johannesburg!', followed immediately by 'Hello, South Africa!' No wonder they call themselves Foreigner.

(4) Profound Sociopolitical Observations. While most people go to rock concerts to get away from politics, rock stars are not so easily disabused of their responsibility as spokespersons for a generation. Foreigner's Mick Jones did his bit by noting the great social and political changes that had finally paved the way for Foreigner to visit South Africa, concluding with the classic battle-cry of the rock 'n roll spokesperson: 'Long live rock 'n roll, baby!'

(5) 'Are you feeling all right? Are you having a good time?' Repeated a minimum of three times, because the audience's answer is somehow never convincing enough to begin with.

(6) The Fifteen Minute Drum Solo. A mandatory interlude, designed to give the rest of the band a much-needed opportunity to meditate, make a phone call, swig a mineral water, and do whatever else rock stars do backstage while the drummer is going bananas up front.

(7) The Atrocious Bass Guitar Solo. Bass guitars were not designed as solo instruments, but someone's got to keep things cooking while the drummer retires backstage.

(8) Cunningly Camouflaged Introductions to Greatest Hits. When you've played the same song 352 times in the

last six months, you want to make it sound a little different this time round. So you pretend you're not going to play it. And then you play it. The audience goes wild, mercifully obscuring the fact that you've forgotten the words to the chorus again.

(9) People Waving Cigarette Lighters In the Air. Origins obscure, but believed to stem from Baby, You Can Light My Fire by The Doors, or villagers storming the castle with blazing torches in the Frankenstein movies.

(10) Giant Inflatable Props. At the end of Jukebox Heroes, Foreigner's final song of the evening, a giant jukebox slowly inflates itself in the darkness, rising to full height as a battery of white lights illuminates everyone's watches and reminds them that it's almost time to go see whether their car radios have been stolen yet. Long live rock 'n roll, baby!

THE MAN WHO FELT LIKE A MILLION BUCKS

At 10.30 am on a bright and sunny Monday morning, just in time for tea, the Executive Director of the megalithic financial corporation nosed his gunmetal-coloured Mercedes down the corrugated parking ramp of the quartz-and-sandstone skyscraper known as Bankers' Trust House.

His radial tyres slithered and squealed on the oil-stained concrete floor, but he quickly drowned out the sound by side-swiping a couple of the dazzling white Toyota Corolla 1300s he had authorised as an austerity measure for middle-management. Like an ocean liner coming in to dock, the Executive Director cruised into the bay that bore his numberplate, coming to a halt with a satisfying thump of titanium on rubber.

He slammed the door and jabbed his thumb on the immobiliser button. Instantly, the Merc flashed its indicators and emitted a single electronic blip. This simple ritual always invested the Executive Director with a sudden surge of unstoppable personal power.

He was good at immobilising gestures, and could freeze a middle-manager across an open-plan office with just one extended finger. But naked power was not all that he craved. As he strode to the lifts, the Executive Director smiled softly to himself and took a deep whiff of the scent of money that always seemed to permeate into the very bowels of Bankers' Trust House.

'I feel like a million bucks today,' he thought to himself, and then he stopped in his tracks. 'No, wait a second. Maybe I should settle for four hundred and seventy-five thousand.'

After all, times were not as sweet as they used to be in the South African financial marketplace. The downturn was still bottoming out of its most recent plateau, and the Group had just posted a three per cent drop in operating profits over the previous financial year.

He blamed the Government and the ANC for creating a climate of such political and economic instability, that the prime lending rate could drop by 3,75 percentage points in less than three years. For a Group that went out of its way to exhibit social responsibility by loaning capital to people who wanted to buy their own properties or start their own businesses, that meant millions of bucks in interest down the drain.

On top of everything else, the amalgamation was swallowing up a lot more money and manpower than had

'Won't be long ... I'm just off to the Bahamas for a seminar
on Management Ethics.'

initially been bargained for, even if the process of transition had created the opportunity for his scheme and the mechanics for getting away with it. Still, a million at one go did seem a little excessive. Perhaps even unpatriotic.

For now, he would run with the lower option, bearing in mind the words that had been drummed into his psyche during his MBA course dozens of financial years ago.

'Less now,' the desk-thumping Professor had insisted, 'for much more later.' Come to think of it, that was all the Executive Director had ever got out of his MBA. He couldn't, for instance, remember a thing about Corporate Ethics. Had there even been a class in Corporate Ethics?

His dozy ruminations on the subject were interrupted by the sight of a newly appointed administrative assistant floozing into the office and landing a pile of DD-45 Loan Agreement Schedules on his blotter-pad. He looked up and nodded his thanks. She had a figure like a million bucks.

But he wasn't going to play in that ballpark ever again. His mind was now focused on business, not pleasure, as he prepared to demonstrate to himself that they really are one and the same thing. As the Group's Executive Director, he had the advantage of knowing that the buck did not actually stop on his Pledge-waxed mahogany desk.

But on its relentless journey down the plushly carpeted, artwork-lined corridor, it paused long enough for him to squeeze it for all it was worth. Why shouldn't he be rich? Not retirement-annuity rich, not expense-account rich, but cigar-lighting, Moët-quaffing, man-of-means rich, like the people he had to do business with every day.

He knew the most intimate secrets of their balance sheets, and he knew that they hadn't become rich by sitting around waiting for money to fall into their laps. They were self-made men. So he stared at the glowing green figures on his computer monitor, and he decided to make himself a loan of R475 000.

A paltry sum, payable to an insignificant closed corporation of which he was the sole director. Loan Approved. He tapped in the six figures, and his index finger hovered for a moment over the Enter button. Deep inside the antechambers of his conscience, a seed of doubt was beginning to take root.

He was aware that what he was about to do was unethical, illegal, and immoral. But was it really wrong? After all, everyone out there was doing it. Civil servants, stockbrokers, homeland ministers. It was true that two wrongs didn't make a right. But they did set a precedent.

Anyway, he was a firm believer in the entrepreneurial spirit, and it seemed to him that the activity in which he was about to engage fitted every definition of risk-taking, courage, and innovation. Inside his grey suit, behind his discreetly striped tie, he had always seen himself that way. An entrepreneur.

Suffused with sudden revelation, he took a deep breath and pressed the backspace key to erase all trace of the R475 000. Then he typed in R1 200 000 and pressed Enter. Much better. Ithuba Scratchcards, the Executive Director thought fondly to himself, are for the little people.

Over the next few months, the Executive Director added modest amounts to his portfolio, and although he could finally call himself a rich man, he never let it stand in the way of his work. Indeed, a personally signed memo from the Managing Director commended him for his initiative and commitment to a special project aimed at increasing counter charges on all transactions involving amounts under R10 000.

The Executive Director did not let it go to his head. He was just doing his job. With interest. Then, one Friday afternoon at 4.30 pm, when everyone from Chief Assistant Auditor up was getting ready for Scotch and Soda in the boardroom, the Managing Director called an urgent meeting in his own cavernous office. No drinks.

'Gentlemen,' he said, 'I'll get straight to the point. I am concerned that a culture of fraud is beginning to take root in our organisation.'

As a cloak of silence fell upon the room, the Executive Director developed a sudden acute awareness of the mechanics of involuntary action. Swallowing. Breathing. Blinking. The circulation of blood. He thought he had taken everything into account. But he had never for a moment considered the possibility of being found out. What for? They were just loans, for heaven's sake. He was always going to pay them back. With interest.

When he was able to think, the one thought that ransacked his brain was: Who did it? Who ratted on me? Instinctively, his gaze shifted to the Chief Assistant Auditor, a small, meticulous man of irreproachable integrity and high moral standards. The bastard.

He looked away and seemed to cower, and the Executive Director felt himself burning under the irony of it all, for he had given this sanctimonious ferret the job in the first place. But he wasn't going to take it lying down. He wasn't going to just sit there and ... the Managing Director spoke.

'Yesterday, at our Village East sub-branch,' he said, opening a pale yellow folder, 'a junior waste-clerk admitted to fraudulently transferring a sum of R22 500 into a

48

transmission account in the name of a male associate, believed to be her boyfriend. The day before, at Maddison Street West, a revolving debit order clerk of two years' standing was found to have appropriated more than R56 000 in an elaborate scam involving the feeding and clearing of three Automatic Teller Machines in the vicinity of the branch. And just today, gentlemen, not more than 30 minutes ago, I learned from the manager of one of our biggest branches in the northern Orange Free State that . . .'

With a skill perfected over years on the corporate social circuit, the Executive Director managed to transform his guffaw into a wracking cough before anyone could deny him the benefit of the doubt. He toyed with the figures as they fluttered from the sanctuary of the folder: R20 000, R42 000, R65 000, R17 500, R76 000 . . . petty cash! That was the trouble with the country today. People had no ambition. It was up to the entrepreneurs to keep things moving. A homily from a time-planning seminar leaped into his mind: 'Make no little plans. They have no magic to stir men's blood.'

The folder flapped shut, and the Managing Director leaned forward with fire in his eyes. 'I want to make it absolutely clear,' he said, 'that we will not tolerate this kind of rot and corruption in our organisation. I, personally, will see to it that prosecution follows in every single case of suspected fraud or misappropriation, no matter how insignificant the amount or junior the employee. Now let's have something to drink, dammit.'

The Executive Director nodded grim assent. He had two Scotch and Sodas and a handful of salted peanuts, and then he drove straight home, where big, blood-stirring plans kept him from falling asleep until well after midnight.

The end, when it came, was neither swift nor dramatic. It was dull, discreet, pained with exaggerated politeness. Disappointment and dashed illusions strained the air in the boardroom, and the only moment of tension arose during a sharp exchange of semantics over the difference between 'theft' and 'unauthorised loan'.

The Chief Assistant Auditor presented him with an affidavit, and he signed every page on the top-right and lower-left corners, in gold-nibbed Shaeffer fountain-pen. The best that money can buy. He handed over the keys to the Merc without waiting to be asked, but the Chief Assistant Auditor said it was OK, he could just leave them with the chauffeur.

'I am sorry,' said the Chief Assistant Auditor, in the lift down to B1. 'I hope you can understand I was only doing my job.' Of course, grunted the Executive Director, but he was the one who was really feeling sorry. This poor man, this bureaucrat, would never know what it felt like to be rich. Would never know the magic of big plans to stir men's blood. Would never know danger. 'Can I offer you a friendly word of advice?' the Chief Assistant Auditor whispered. 'Get a good lawyer.'

At home, stripped of his tie and his office, the Executive Director watched television and read the papers. What really boiled his blood was the way he was suddenly being singled out as a symbol of the moral decay at the core of South African society, as if all the years of greed and looting and Apartheid were his fault alone.

The word 'alleged' was used in a snide, grudging way, and the most absurd sums were being mentioned; nowhere near the truth. He felt insulted, belittled. Whatever happened to justice? Right of reply? The simple, everyday ethical norms and standards of his generation? It was shocking. Enough to make you want to leave the country.

He got a good lawyer, who was prepared to proclaim his innocence and protect his interests for a cash consideration upfront. And then he left the country. In London, after a visit to a conveniently chosen branch of Lloyds Bank, he settled in well, issuing a statement through his lawyer that he would not be returning to South Africa for the foreseeable future. Still, every now and again, he felt a little like Salman Rushdie. It's a small world. You can't put anything past some people.

So he was not really surprised, one night in the Coach and Horses in Putney, when he locked eyes with a familiar face from a distant time and country. He was simply immobilised with fear and loathing, because the face belonged to the Chief Assistant Auditor from Bankers' Trust House in Johannesburg. He tried to run. But he couldn't hide.

'Hello,' said the Chief Assistant Auditor. The Executive Director slowly unfroze. 'Look,' he said, 'I don't know how you found me here, but I want to warn you not to try anything. This is England, not South Africa.' The Chief Assistant Auditor smiled. 'I know. That's why I'm here.'

There was a moment of stunned silence, and then the Pound Sterling dropped. They slapped each other on the back, bought each other drinks, and spoke about business and South Africa long into the night. But they're not coming back. These days, you know, there's just too much damn competition.

PLEASE BE PATIENT, WE'RE HAVING A CIVIL WAR

The delegates streamed out of the conference hall at two o'clock in the morning, their faces bleached and drawn in the nicotine-filtered glare of the television lights. At last, after months of intense negotiation, on the eve of the country's first democratic elections, they had reached full and unequivocal consensus. The talks were off. So were the elections.

From now on, they said, fists clenched, jaws set in iron, there was only one way out of the impasse, only one way towards the new social and political order. War.

The word fell like a mortar on the banks of thrusting microphones, but even as the foreign correspondents bolted for their satellite feeds — it had just gone 6 pm in Atlanta — there was very little of what you would actually call surprise.

Even in the distant, rosy-tinted days of Codesa I and II, war had always been somewhere on the constitutional agenda, politely preceded by 'civil' and evoked as the ultimate South African nightmare by any delegate who believed his or her submissions were not being taken seriously.

But no one had really bothered to break the threat — or the promise — down to its practical, everyday implications. For one thing, if there was to be a war in South Africa, whose war would it be? The Third Boer War of General Eugene Terre'Blanche and his khaki-clad horsemen of the Apocalypse?

The People's Revolution of APLA and its balaclava-camouflaged band of freelance gun-slingers? Winnie Mandela's bush-war? Mangosuthu Buthelezi's secession option? The final hurrah of the SADF and its small army of otherwise unemployed teenage conscripts?

In any case, how would anyone be able to tell the difference between full-scale war and normal, everyday life in South Africa? It was all too complicated to contemplate, so everyone just holstered their weapons and settled for soliloquies of peace.

But the war-talk continued, inside and outside the negotiation chamber, at marches, at rallies, on Agenda with John Bishop. Then people got tired of talking.

'It's War!' screamed the Sunday Times banner-posters one crisp autumn morning, in what many people took to be a reference to the sending-off of five South African players during the second test at Twickenham.

But the truth really began to sink in when the State President, looking tired yet somehow serene, addressed the nation in a live television broadcast from Uruguay later that evening.

He said he would be flying home as soon as circumstances permitted, and in the mean time, he wished to assure all South Africans that they would continue to receive the kind of leadership they had come to expect from the Government during this time of crisis. Then the screen went black.

Across the country, people who were able to maintain a rational frame of mind took it for a simple power failure. But it wasn't. It was a success. So much so, that the duty reporter at SAPA took six calls from different Liberation Army spokesmen claiming responsibility for the well-planned and executed act of sabotage on the SABC's central transmitter.

It was only later, when a flustered continuity announcer appeared on air to explain that the blackout had been caused by industrial action at the SABC — just a few days before, the head of the technical workers' union had declared war on management — that some semblance of order began to return to the situation. But by then it was too late. The real war had begun.

At the Union Buildings in Pretoria, lights blazed into the night as the Cabinet and its Generals met to consider an early end to the hostilities. But all hopes faded just before midnight, when the Generals stormed out of the room after yet another blistering row over Defence Force budget cuts, manpower and equipment shortages, and the early curtailment of conscription.

There was silence for a moment, and then the Acting State President shrugged his shoulders and identified the upside. 'Well, at least that seems to rule out the possibility of a military coup.'

Of course, there were other armies, other Generals, other soldiers awaiting orders. In Ventersdorp, Command HQ of the Afrikaner Weerstandsbeweging's land, sea, and air forces, an aide spread a thin layer of resin-based glue over the General's saddle before he rode out to address his troops on the eve of battle.

It was the moment they had been waiting for since 1910. The beginning of the Third War of Freedom. Already, most of Ventersdorp was under their command. Soon, they would sweep across the land and recapture Potchefstroom, Brandfort, Piet Retief, Bloemfontein, Vryheid, Pretoria . . . soon, the old republics of Transvaal, the Orange Free State, and northern Natal would once again be safely in Boer hands.

Then, when the smoke had settled and the boundaries had been redrawn, they would rise up proudly and do the only sensible thing. Declare war on the rest of the country.

In the quiet backstreets of Soweto, meanwhile, a South African Defence Force Hippo lumbered in and out of the potholes, its halogen eyes piercing the smouldering darkness. Inside, alert, disciplined, ready for war, the commander of the under-14 wing of the local branch of the Azanian People's Liberation Army peered over the steering-wheel while his lieutenant worked the pedals.

Only the day before, the Hippo, with less than 13 000 km on the clock, had been liberated from its previous owners, a light-infantry detachment of the African National Congress's Youth League.

The troops themselves, responding to a call from a loose coalition of progressive political organisations, had already pulled out of the townships, and were now positioning themselves at strategic locations in and around the suburbs of Johannesburg.

A ring of steel was thrown around Sandton City, Cresta Centre, and the Fourways Mall, but by the time the soldiers got to Eastgate, it was too late. Hundreds of thousands of rands worth of merchandise had already been looted, although it was clear that the total would have been much higher if most of the centre's shopping trolleys had not already been lying at the bottom of Bruma Lake.

But one thing was certain. War had come to the suburbs of South Africa, and the country would never be the same. Helicopter gunships flew low in the night sky, their throbbing rotors setting off car and house alarms, their powerful searchlights shining through the acrid smoke of countless backyard braais. It was Sunday night. There was nothing to watch on TV.

But with the dawn came the first real wave of panic, as hundreds of South Africans of all political persuasions

stormed their neighbourhood shopping centres in search of essential commodities.

There were scenes of desperation and pandemonium as gunshop-owner after gunshop-owner double-bolted his security doors and put up hand-scrawled signs reading 'Sorry, Sold Out', 'Closed Due to Emergency Stocktaking', and 'Strictly One Box of Bullets Per Customer'.

There was something strangely familiar about that one, but few people seemed to take any notice. In the midst of anarchy and confusion, a ravenous hunger for real, concrete information gripped the land.

But all you could get on the SABC's regional radio stations was a selection of Strauss Waltzes, and John Robbie's slot on 702 had mysteriously been taken over by Dr Petzenwurfer, the resident pet psychologist. When the daily edition of The Star hit the streets, it was sold out in minutes, but all it had to say was 'Gold Soars to $550', alongside a six-column colour picture of the State President receiving the Freedom of Montevideo.

In pubs and offices, on street corners, in block-long queues at petrol stations, people engulfed themselves and each other with wild waves of rumour and innuendo.

The Union Buildings had been occupied by an armoured division of the AWB, who had burst their way through the security checkpoint in a Toyota diesel bakkie. The KwaZulu administration had announced its intention of seceding from Natal, although the Chief Minister was still only halfway through the preface to his opening declaration.

The beleaguered South African Defence Force had been split into two separate camps, one of which didn't even have tents. The streets of the strategic town of Witbank were deserted, following a mass evacuation by local residents. Either that, or it was a Sunday.

Pop megastar Michael Jackson would be staging a 'Peace Concert' in Soweto's Orlando Stadium, which was out of the jurisdiction of the Los Angeles Police Department. The main highway to Jan Smuts Airport had been blocked off with petrol drums, and all outgoing flights had been put on hold. However, international tourists were still welcome.

The truth, as is usually the case, was somewhat less sensational. The country was still firmly under Government control, even if the Cabinet had been obliged to temporarily relocate its headquarters from the Union Buildings to an underground bunker somewhere in the Kalahari.

In his cavernous office, adjacent to a wine cellar that was generously stocked with crates of Allesverloren Red, the Acting State President was on the hotline to President Bill Clinton of the USA. President Clinton, double-checking the map in his Oval Office, said he was deeply concerned about the crisis in South Africa, and would not hesitate to second a detachment of US Marines from Somalia to restore hope and keep the peace.

The offer was politely declined, on the grounds that there were already enough people running around shooting. What would be appreciated, at this stage, was a clear acknowledgement by the Clinton Administration that the South African Government was still running the country, and that the minor territorial gains by Liberation Armies on the extreme left and right were strictly temporary.

As a token of good faith, the Acting State President gave the assurance that he would not authorise the use of nuclear force unless it became absolutely necessary.

Beyond the multi-insulated doors of the Kalahari bunker, meanwhile, things were getting slightly out of hand. Johannesburg was under the control of a thirtysomething splinter faction of the ANC Youth League, and a curfew had been placed on the Central Business District, in terms of which anyone found wandering the streets between 6 pm and 6 am was liable to be assaulted and robbed of his valuables.

Running artillery battles occupied most of the daylight hours, although the armoured vehicles and tanks of the SADF were no real match for the minibus taxis. The price of gold shot beyond the psychological barrier of $650 an ounce, and flak-jacketed stockbrokers were earning commissions unheard of since the middle Eighties. In Main Street, several historic sandstone buildings were reduced to rubble by the fighting, unexpectedly saving Anglo American the cost of implosion.

In Pretoria, which was still firmly under the control of the Civil Service, the grounds of the British Embassy were under siege, with fully laden helicopters battling to take off from the roof, and hundreds of people shouting 'I'm British! I'm British!' at the heavy wrought-iron gates.

In Cape Town, which was under the control of 350 schoolchildren from Mitchell's Plain, people were advised to avoid the city centre unless they had urgent business to attend to. The city was deserted.

Deep beneath the sands of the Kalahari, the Acting State President poured himself another glass of Allesverloren and wondered where it had all gone wrong. There was so much hope in the air that distant February, so much back-slapping camaraderie between once-bitter enemies, so much faith and resolve in the slow but steady process of delaying the implementation of a genuine democracy. But people were so impatient. So hungry for power. So ... the telephone rang.

The Acting State President picked up the receiver and accepted a call that instantly froze his blood. Ashen-faced, he put the phone down, rose from his chair, and broke the news to his Cabinet colleagues. They stood in stunned silence, jaws agape, clenching and unclenching their fists to keep their circulation going. Something had to be done. Immediately.

Two days later, the Government and accredited representatives of 26 warring parties and organisations sat down at the World Trade Centre in Kempton Park to sign a document guaranteeing the immediate cessation of hostilities on all fronts, the restoration of democratic elections and Constitutional negotiations, and an independent judicial inquiry into the demands for a separate Afrikaner Volkstaat.

This time, when the delegates faced the cameras, they were smiling, and the smoke that filtered the lights was from their own Havana cigars. Then someone shouted 'We'd better hurry', and the people whose awesome task it was to determine the future of South Africa were ushered into a private screening room for the live transmission of the third and final rugby test between South Africa and England. It was a small price to pay. Hell, who needs war?

TRAVEL

THE SOUND OF CAGED BIRDS SINGING

I flew from Johannesburg to Hong Kong, flew from Hong Kong to Beijing, checked into the Hotel Kunlun, poured myself a cup of green herbal tea, and fell asleep before I could drink it. When I awoke, it was to the sound of ringing bells, cutting across continents and time-zones and the gulf of my subconscious. I stumbled over to the window, pulled open the curtains, and there it was. The People's Republic of China, at rush-hour.

It was the most utilitarian vision of democracy I had ever seen: One Person, One Bicycle. And in the middle of it all, coughing smoke, a broken-down bus. The cyclists flowed around it, like water round a rock. Every now and again, an old Army truck or a cannibalised pre-war tractor would putt-putt out of an unguarded intersection, and the front rank of cyclists would swerve and judder and avoid it by the skin of their tyres.

I took a look at Beijing. It had come a long way since 900 000 BC, when Peking Man discovered fire. Now Beijing Man had worked out a way to keep it going. There were smokestacks and turbines and generators all over the place, and yellow-beaked cranes roosting like gargoyles on half-completed buildings. Twilight crowned the pollution with a halo of rust, and I followed some of the little tributaries as they eased from the shallows of the stream on to the shore.

The housing complexes across the road looked like multistorey car parks, only not as luxurious. I looked into some of the units, and saw shadows moving in the dim green light. On the balcony of one apartment, suspended in a bamboo cage, a white dove was flapping its wings, like a canary in a coalmine. Then I swept my gaze across to the curved tower of the Hotel Kunlun, which was reserved for Foreign Guests of the Chinese People.

It was getting brighter and brighter, chandeliers shining like jewels in the lobby, lights going on in every suite and corridor. The hotel was like an incubus, sucking up electricity from the fizzing neon filaments of the housing-blocks. I took a sip of green herbal tea. It tasted like tobacco in bathwater. Then I rushed to catch the lift, because I didn't want to miss the evening's performance of Chinese Acrobatics at the International Club in Beijing.

As I took my seat, four small boys with Army haircuts were hurling Ming vases at each other. The vases criss-crossed through the air, landing with a hollow clang on foreheads, rolling down necks, over shoulders, down backs, up outstretched arms, and into the air with a half-twist and a double-somersault. Then a girl with pigtails bent over backwards on an ironing-board, and people placed a pyramid of wineglasses on her forehead, and bowls of water on her palms and the soles of her feet. Squinting at the wineglasses, she corkscrewed slowly round, without spilling a drop. There were tumblers and jugglers and conjurers, and people diving through hula-hoops simultaneously from opposite directions, missing each other by a gasp and a heartbeat.

But slowly, here and there, little things started to go wrong. An elbow brushed the inside of a chain of hula-hoops, and the whole delicately balanced construction came tumbling down. A China plate spinning on the point of a steel rod wobbled drunkenly and fell to the table. Fragile objects slipped from the orbit of jugglers, and a gymnast somersaulted from a springboard, misjudged his velocity, and overshot the shoulders of another gymnast. But the acrobats and the magicians picked themselves up, smiled, and started all over again, as if nothing had happened.

The next morning, as sleet drifted from Beijing's grey skies, turning to soot before it hit the ground, I took a walk around the Square of the Gate of Heavenly Peace. Tiananmen. It was a vast, treeless plain, designed for military parades rather than casual lunchtime strolls, but the People's Liberation Army was having an off-day, and apart from a few hundred tourists and the odd Youth Brigade platoon on a field trip, I had the place to myself.

Chairman Mao's mausoleum was behind me, and his fat, smiling portrait was across the road, and all around were the concrete bunkers of government and the windswept martyrs of the Revolution, frozen in bronze with their AK-47s. So I stood in the middle of Tiananmen Square, where the Army met the students on June 4, 1989, and the Army won. There were conflicting reports, but I knew what really happened, because I had picked up a little blue booklet in the hotel lobby: 'Report on Checking the Turmoil and Quelling the Counter-Revolutionary Rebellion'.

It appeared that a tiny handful of anti-government agitators, including 'hooligans, ruffians, and ex-convicts who did not turn over a new leaf' had conspired to overthrow the leadership of the Chinese Communist Party and subvert the people's democratic dictatorship. As a result, more than 6 000 casualties were suffered in the ranks of the People's Liberation Army, and at least 1 280 military vehicles, police cars, and public buses were destroyed by the tiny handful.

'Among the non-military casualties,' said the report, 'were rioters who deserved the punishment.' It was quiet in the square, and I watched a proud father taking a photograph of his infant son, who was wearing a full PLA uniform with red and gold braid and a peaked cap swimming around his ears. Behind him, the Monument to the People's Heroes seemed to sway beneath the clouds.

In Xian, the ancient capital of China, I met a student named Li Hai Yi. We were walking through the open-air food market, where ducks and chickens were being roasted with their heads still connected to their bodies, when Li Hai suddenly pointed to the night sky and declared, 'I believe in God!' It sounded like a pretty subversive statement to me, so I asked him what he meant. But he just shrugged his shoulders, gave a Chinese smile, and said: 'Maybe God can make me rich.'

Personal wealth is China's new fringe religion, an offshoot of the Mother Church that offers salvation through informal free enterprise. In theory, it's the crux of China's bold new economic reform policy. In practice, it's hundreds of people standing at the side of the road, selling farm goods and folk handicrafts and keeping the after-tax profits for themselves. These free markets and private businesses are the most vital sign of the widening of the parameters of Chinese Socialism. On the other hand, maybe they're just a natural by-product of the macro-economic retrenchment process.

I asked Li Hai Yi, who was studying environmental control at the Xian Institute of Metallurgy and Construction Engineering, what he would buy if God made him rich. He told me about the Four Bigs: refrigerator, washing machine, television set, tape-recorder. Then we got on to the other numbers. In China, ideas, philosophies, plans, goals, and policies are always rounded up and regimented into little number-squads for ease of reference and recitation. There are the Five Things to Emphasise: Decorum, Manners, Hygiene, Discipline, and High Morals. There are the Four Things to Beautify: Mind, Language, Behaviour, and Environment. There are the Three Things to Love: Socialism, the Motherland, and the Communist Party of China.

Li Hai Yi was clicking up the numbers on an abacus in the general goods store where he worked every evening in Xian. Business was quiet, except for the clicking, so he decided the time had come to beautify his mind a little. 'What is the gross national product of South Africa?' he asked, squinting behind his bifocals. I said I'd have to get back to him on that, and when I took out my pen, he suddenly leaped from his chair and offered me a stubby Chinese pencil. I said, no thanks, I've got a pen. But he insisted, and I realised he was trying to do a swap. So I gave him the pen. It was just a regular Maruzen felt-tip, R3 plus tax at any branch of the CNA. But Li Hai Yi stared at the felt-tip, as if it was a diamond, and he began writing things down on the palm of his hand.

'Apartheid'. 'Mandela'. 'Plum Blossoms'. 'Budgerigar'. 'Springbok'. 'Coat of Arms'. When I shook Li Hai Yi's hand, it was covered with spidery scratchings, and mine was empty. Back at the hotel, I watched a movie on the state television channel. Chinese soldiers were harassing Chinese workers in a big steel factory. The workers stood tall and glared, metal bouncing light off their faces. One of the workers picked up a monkey-wrench, turning it over and over in his fist. The soldiers dropped their jaws and took a couple of steps back. No one said anything. Other workers began picking up tools. A soldier fired a bullet into the air. The workers advanced. The officer in charge screamed an order. And then, on the verge of the revolution, I fell asleep.

It was early the next morning, on the way to see the Terracotta Army of the Emperor Qin Shi Huangdi, that I first began to notice things were missing. It wasn't just the conspicuous absence of graffiti or advertising on the walls of the cities. It was the natural landscape: there was hardly a blade of grass, or a bird in the sky, or an insect on the ground. There was just this eerie, hermetically sealed stillness in the atmosphere, and I began to wonder if I was still on the same planet. I asked Zhang Xiaoming, of the China International Travel Service, and he said previous campaigns to eliminate pests and invaders from the countryside had proved highly successful.

A few years ago, peasants across China had been advised to go out into the fields, banging pots and pans for hours on end. The idea was to frighten off the sparrows and blackbirds, and it worked; the birds began dropping from the sky. Then there was the campaign against grass, which was considered to be unhealthy because it provided refuge for snakes and insects. So, all across China, at grassroots level, grass was plucked out by the roots. Zhang Xiaoming laughed 'Of course, things are changing now,' he said. And he pointed out a clump of wild grass on the roadside, and, high in the skeleton branches of a fir tree, a bird's scraggly nest.

We passed a field of pomegranate trees, heavy with swollen-bellied fruit. Zhang said pomegranates were a traditional Chinese symbol of fertility. That was the problem. Too many people were eating too many pomegranates. Despite fifteen years of the most intensive population control programme in the world, featuring financial incentives, peer and Party pressure, free contraceptives and an official acknowledgement that one in three Chinese pregnancies ends in abortion, the national goal of a 1,2-billion population limit by the year 2000 seems more and more like a demographer's crazy dream. Officially, couples who exceed the one-child limit are subject to strict ideological censure and the denial of health and education benefits for the surplus child. Unofficially, you only have to visit a Chinese kindergarten to see precisely where bureaucracy and social engineering begin to collide with human nature.

Chinese babies, eyes as black as olives, cheeks as fat and red as pomegranates, never seem to bawl in public. Buoyed by bright, plump nylon anoraks, they just stand there, wobbling slightly, quiet and wise as sages. When they turn around, you notice they aren't wearing nappies, but woollen trousers split like a crescent moon from the waist. The Chinese invented gunpowder, printing, paper currency, paddle-boats, wheelbarrows, and the navigational compass, and the West wasted no time in lifting the patents. But somehow, despite their practical ingenuity and environmental friendliness, split-bottomed baby-trousers have yet to bridge the Great Cultural Gap.

In the lobby of the Dragon Hotel in Hangzhou, I met Frank Archibald, an Australian. He was the Western partner in a joint industrial venture with the Chinese government, and while he admitted to an incomplete understanding of Chinese culture and business practice, he understood the bottom line only too well. 'No bloody unions,' he drawled, ordering another beer. Archibald's line of business was

Ginseng soap, in particular a variety that claimed to banish menstrual cramps. That was for the export market.

Archibald said his factory workers took home 200 Yuan a month — about R100 — for an eight-hour day. They were constitutionally forbidden to strike, unless their national honour was offended. Archibald had discovered this little caveat the day after Australia's Foreign Affairs Minister made a public statement critical of China's policy towards Tibet. When his workers downed tools and switched off their machines, Archibald phoned the Australian embassy in rage and panic. They said there was only one thing he could do: the Chinese Thing. So he stood before his workers, bowed his head, and accepted personal responsibility for the Foreign Minister's indiscretion. And everybody went back to making soap.

At the Hangzhou Silk Printing and Dyeing Complex, I watched women dipping their fingers into vats of steaming water, lifting out cocoons and unravelling the soggy threads on old wooden looms. At the end of the line, instead of butterflies, there were silk blouses. I caught the train to Shanghai. Outside the window, industry and agriculture rushed headlong into one another, smokestacks blurring into rice-paddies, groaning water-barges colliding with fields of yellow rapeseed. At last, I knew what was really missing from the Chinese landscape, rural, urban, industrial. Empty space.

This was especially so in Shanghai, where you could hardly move for hustlers and sailors and sidewinding characters whispering 'Change money?' in the shadows. There was an edge to the city, with its oil-slicked waterfront and its old sandstone buildings evacuated by the colonial bureaucrats. It was Shanghai, after all, and it had a reputation to live down to. So, in the Rainbow Hotel, which looked swish and classy from the outside, I was almost relieved to find an unmade bed, strange, dark stains on the carpet, and holes punched in the chipboard in the bathroom. I liked the place, because it had standards.

'No guest is allowed to up anyone for the night, or let anyone use his/her own bed in the hotel,' warned the Hotel Regulations, which had been compiled by the Shanghai Public Security Bureau. 'No birds, domestic animals, or other unsnairy articles are allowed to be brought into the hotel,' added Regulation Number Four. The next day, on an official tour of the July First Commune on the outskirts of Shanghai, I wandered down the tunnel-like corridors of a health care centre that served the commune's 18 000 inhabitants. The place smelled of dry rot, steamed rice, and disinfectant, and there was a poster on the wall of a giant rat in a circle with a line drawn through it. Opposite, there was an oil painting of the Great Wall of China, set in a landscape of deep, dark jade, the colour of madness.

Women waited with their babies on hard wooden benches, and in a dustbin on top of the stairs, I caught a glimpse of old dressings and an empty drip and several other unsnairy articles. An old man was sitting in a chair in a doctor's surgery, smiling serenely as the doctor stuck ash-tipped needles into pressure points on the old man's thighs and biceps. Then the doctor passed a couple of wooden tubes through a methylated flame, and they sucked on the old man's flesh like leeches. The doctor returned to his desk and scribbled out a prescription in Chinese. It looked like every other doctor's prescription I ever saw.

In Guilin, on the border between China and Vietnam, the weather was not miserable, merely inscrutable. I was standing on the prow of a flat-bottomed ferry as it belched and bellowed down the Li River, past paddies and furrows where peasants in black pyjamas drove water buffaloes through the rich black mud. There were conical peaks wherever you looked, giant stalagmites coated with clumps of steamy moss and wrapped in layers of gauze. High on a cragface, where dragons and serpents lurked, I saw a pterodactyl flap its leathery wings. But it was only a cormorant, looking out for fish.

If Hong Kong is a pot of boiling milk and honey, then Guangzhou, two hours away by train, laps up the overflow. It's one big, throbbing free market, full of jutting flatblocks and cocky entrepreneurs, and almost as many cars as bicycles. The supermarket windows are crammed with bright clothes and flickering television sets, and at the Qin Jing market, you can buy a puppy in a cage, or have it boiled in a pot while you wait. Early in the morning, on my last day in China, I took a stroll through the People's Park on Shamian Island, overlooking the Pearl River. It was rush-hour.

People were pushing their bicycles on to the ferries, and the air was thick with smoke and hooting. In the park, between the fish-pond and the rock-garden, people were limbering up in slow, silent motion, clawing and kicking at the empty space around them. It was Tai Chi, an aerobic version of Kung Fu, and it was easy to see why you were supposed to do it outdoors. Further back, under the weeping willow trees, little knots of old men were sitting on their haunches, smoking hand-rolled cigarettes. They were watching birds in bamboo cages. There were bicycle bells and hooters and foghorns all around, but all you could hear, at rush-hour in the People's Republic of China, was the sound of caged birds singing.

I'VE BEEN TO SOWETO, I'M BACK

Every weekday morning at a quarter to nine, not always on the dot, a white minibus pulls up outside the Carlton Hotel in Johannesburg, and eight or nine people climb inside for a journey to another country. Soweto. City within a city; festering symbol of despair and defiance; R25 per person for a four-hour guided tour, tea and biscuits included.

'Good morning, everybody, my name is Bushy,' announces a smiling young woman in the comfort and safety of our unmarked vehicle. She is wearing a daisy-yellow summer dress and lots of purple blusher on her cheeks. Radiating effervescent enthusiasm, she instantly blots out the shadow of unease that hangs over the place she calls home. But that is exactly why we have come.

To see the real Soweto. To get a truly balanced picture. To see a workshop for the disabled. To visit a traditional African village. To get a panoramic view from the top of the Oppenheimer Tower. To see Soweto, as far as the eye can see.

'People are desperate to get to Soweto,' says Bushy, pointing at a cluster of flustered and frustrated tourists lining the Carlton's red carpet. The minibus will return for them in the afternoon.

Clunk. The sliding door slams shut, and we head for the conglomeration of 26 dormitory townships spread over 100 square kilometres on the south-western side of Johannesburg. Our driver's name is Silela. It is a Sotho word, meaning 'to cry'.

Every month, Bushy tells us, smiling sweetly, there are more than 3 000 accidents involving minibus taxis on their way to or from South Africa's black townships. Competition for passengers is intense, forcing drivers to drive very fast, stop without warning, turn without indicating, and change lanes without looking as they make their way to pick up or drop off another paying fare.

'We will be all right?' asks the Italian woman, tapping Bushy softly on the shoulder as she cocks her head at Silela. 'Oh yes,' says Bushy. 'He is not allowed to drive very fast. Otherwise, you won't see Soweto.'

There are eight of us in the minibus today. The Italian woman has a creaky accent and hair like a flame lily. She lives in Johannesburg, 30 years now. Twenty-five times she has been to Soweto. The first time, it cost her three rands. Her sister, blonde, and her brother-in-law, black-haired and shrugging, have come from Italy to visit. No English.

The biology teacher from Alabama, wearing corduroys and velskoene, is talking gently about African culture. 'When they raise both hands in greeting, it's a sign of respect.' He raises both hands in greeting, like a man trying to ward off a nuclear attack.

The woman behind the sunglasses is from California, where she breeds horses. The man in the lime golf shirt and casual slax is a German diplomat from Mozambique. He wears the politely pursed look of an unofficial fact-finder. The female student from Cambridge is pale but serene. The native South African has nothing better to do on a Friday morning. Anyway, you don't want to go into these places on your own.

'The population of Soweto is estimated at two and a half million people, although the official figure stands at one and a half million people. The reason for this discrepancy is the large number of unregistered people living in Soweto.' Bushy pauses, signalling the Italian woman to translate for her relatives.

On our left there is a mine dump, a slab of dry custard covered with weeds. On our right there is a minibus, but not for long. We ease off the motorway, our attention briefly diverted by the headquarters of the South African Permanent Building Society, an Aztec pyramid with goosebumps of gravel.

' . . . dug holes in the ground and used them as lavatories. And so bubonic plague broke out in 1904, and a commission recommended that blacks be moved out of Johannesburg and only allowed in while serving their masters. Coming up on our right, we have the Johannesburg municipal testing station . . .'

I drift off, thinking about the first time I went to Soweto. I was eight years old, in Standard One. It was a school tour to Dobsonville, the last township to the west. The beacons are hazy: the inside of a cinema, a small brown church, an immunisation clinic, nursery school children clapping hands.

But one thing I remember clearly. The fat flapping sound as the tyres of the big school bus rolled slowly over the rails of the level crossing, the border between their place and ours.

We're here. As we cross the threshold into Soweto, Bushy casually holds up a T-shirt, available in small, medium, and large. On the front: I'VE BEEN TO SOWETO. On the back: I'M BACK.

It is a little early in the tour to be thinking seriously about such souvenirs, even at R15 a throw, but Bushy's bubbly confidence is almost enough to make us ignore the sight, coming up on our right, of a policeman with a submachine gun ordering a black man to open the boot of his car.

The pale English student, noticing no commotion, decides to create one. 'What is that soldier doing there?'

This is like asking a person who lives in New York what the Empire State Building is doing there. It is not even a soldier, it is a riot policeman, but such subtleties seem insignificant in the face of the fundamentals. 'What is he looking for?'

Discreetly, Bushy folds the T-shirt and returns it to her bag. 'Hmmm,' she mulls. 'It's just a roadblock. They're looking for . . . stolen cars, drugs, ammunition. Anything.'

The pale English student turns a white shade of pale, but we do not get stopped. Safely inside the borders of Soweto, we pull off on to the shoulder of the road and set foot on the soil of another country. The soil is dry and bony and patched with dead grass, like grazing land after the cows have gone home. Down there, in the crook of the valley, is the railway line that goes to Johannesburg, and beyond, the Golden Highway that goes to Johannesburg, and all around, in brick and mortar and corrugated iron, Soweto. Together, says the poster on the hoarding, we will build a brighter future.

The Italian woman urges her sister and brother-in-law to huddle closer against the backdrop. Snap.

From the wide-angle to the extreme close-up, from the edges of the artery to the heart of darkness. But first, we have to pass through the heart of semi-darkness. Noordgesig, the township for coloureds.

'It is sometimes very difficult to differentiate between a coloured and a white person, and some coloureds are even darker than myself,' explains Bushy, who is the colour of varnished mahogany. 'The only means of telling these darker coloureds apart from the blacks is that they communicate mainly in Afrikaans.'

Now we are in Orlando, where black is black. We stop to look at the people. They are sitting on the stoep of the house on our left. The biology teacher from Alabama raises both hands in greeting. He drops them, softly slapping his thighs. This is a council house, with two rooms and a tiny garage. Which makes three rooms.

WE WON'T PAY RENT! scream the walls in dripping red, while the council hoardings show smiling citizens of Soweto enjoying water and power for the rent they ought to be paying.

'One of the demands of the boycott,' says Bushy, 'is that the council must clean up Soweto. You will notice that it is one of the dirtiest townships you will ever come across.'

She jabs a thumb at the heap of half-burned, dog-bitten rubbish on the corner, next to the vendor who is sourly selling apples and oranges. An old woman, sucking an orange, shuffles up to the minibus and peers inside, smiling mysteriously. The biology teacher does not raise his hands in greeting.

We pass a school: 'Our high schools are characterised by broken windows. Our children do this to take out their frustration over the inferior education they are receiving.' We pass the Orlando Magistrate's Court: 'All our magistrates are white.' We pass the Orlando Police Station: 'Eighty per cent of our police force is black, and twenty per cent is white. The twenty per cent occupy the most senior positions.'

Clearly, the time has come to get a truly balanced picture. We pull into the courtyard of the Orlando Sheltered Workshop, where physically disabled and mentally handicapped Sowetans earn a living by weaving baskets, stringing hammocks, sewing church vestments and spinning rugs, where WORK, according to the manifesto, means PAY, FOOD, CLOTHING, HOUSING SECURITY, AND SELF-RESPECT.

The manager of the workshop steps out to greet us, rubbing his hands in welcome. He is a tall, wiry man with red hair, a pointy beard, and freckles. There is something else about him, and it is the German diplomat who first notices the colour of the Emperor's skin.

'Why is this place managed by a white and not a black?' The pause is pregnant with the sounds of the Orlando Police Station Brass Band, rehearsing a Sousa march in an adjacent hall. Tubas parp, cymbals crash. 'Why not?'

The German diplomat frees a hand from a pocket: 'Because this is Soweto, the home of the black people . . . because it's their country . . .'

'Look,' says the workshop manager, no longer rubbing his hands. 'There is something you have to understand. Many years ago, the Government established a development board to help the people of South-Western Townships become independent. All the specialists, accountants, the engineers, the professional managers, were white. They still are. The blacks still can't manage themselves.'

'Oh, they can't?'

'Show me one country in Africa where the black man manages. Show me one country in Africa where the economy is on a reasonable level. They are all starving! When a black man gets put in charge, there is so much graft and corruption, it's unbelievable.'

Parp. 'Do you not have a counterpart, someone who can take over after a few years maybe?'

Crash. 'How many years? A hundred? A hundred and fifty? Not in my lifetime. Not in his lifetime.'

But then, says the German diplomat, sadly shaking his head, it is useless. 'What is useless?' demands the workshop manager, his voice now rising from irritation to anger. 'The job that I'm doing?'

'Perhaps you are a little frustrated.'

'I'm not frustrated. You're frustrated! You come here, I believe, to have a tour of Soweto, not to ask me political questions. If you want to, I'll talk to you all night about your politics, but at fifty rands an hour, that's my starting fee. And you pay my taxi fare. Uh, ladies and gentlemen, this is our sewing section . . .'

As we wander around the workshop, with the German diplomat at the rear, not sulking but skulking, we learn that you cannot impose first-world standards on third-world people. You have to understand their mindset. You have to provide. The workshop manager says it's Yes, Daddy, No, Daddy; he is not just their manager, he is their father. He shouts above the whacking of weaving-looms, like the sound of cell-doors slamming. A poster on the wall reminds us to pay a visit to the ski-resort of Kitzbühel, next time we're in Austria.

Winnie Mandela? Yes, of course. We have heard a little about her. Now we are going to see her house in Beverly Hills. Built at a cost of R700 000, it is the biggest and most expensive mansion in Soweto. There are 22 rooms.

'Twenty-two rooms!' gasps the pale English student. The house is empty. Squat and trapezoid, a facebrick fortress on a hill of rock, it defeats our closer inspection with gold-tinted windows and a boarded-up gate. We take pictures.

Further down the road, we pass the other home of Winnie Mandela, a red box crowned with barbed wire, and Bushy warns us not to take pictures. There is the house of Archbishop Desmond Tutu. There is the double-storey mansion of Kaizer Motaung, the Big Chief of Sowetan soccer.

This house on the right belongs to a very successful attorney, the only man in Soweto to own a Maserati. Please take a picture.

This burned-out building on our left used to be a beerhall. It was demolished by students in the 1976 riots. Over there is the Nelson Mandela High School, as it is unofficially known, and over there is the Joe Slovo High School.

Spidery graffiti proclaims the battlezones of the Comrades: VIETNAM. RUSSIA. NICARAGUA. WE ARE MARCHING FORWARD TO OUR FREEDOM.

'There is the only Kentucky Fried Chicken in Soweto,' points Bushy, 'and there is Wesbank. As you can see, Soweto is a place of contrasts.'

LIARS, FOOLS, SCEPTICS, AND ATHEISTS, PLEASE KEEP OUT! warns the notice board at the entrance to the traditional African village, but we go in anyway. Even if you don't fall into one or more of these categories to begin with, the process of conversion is automatic.

Here we have dreadlocked sangomas shuffling to a voodoo beat in the shade of a grinning Halloween skull and a Hindu swastika. Here we have a plaster sculpture of a fat blue monster with a red crest running down his back. Here we have a robot man made from scrap metal, guarding the door of a thatched mud hut.

Here we have a lady selling T-shirts: I'VE BEEN TO SOWETO, I'M BACK. Here we have tea and biscuits, and then we climb the Ernest Oppenheimer Tower, 44 storeys high, and we look down on the people of Soweto.

On the way to the kindergarten, we pause to take pictures of Mshengoville, a squatter camp housing 2 000 families in a seething mess of cardboard and corrugated iron. Used to be a golf course. These families share seven communal water taps and a row of blue chemical toilets, but there are stickers on the plywood doors: I LOVE MSHENGOVILLE. A woman on her knees is buffing the stoep of her shack with thick red shoe polish, until it shines like lipstick on a whore.

At the kindergarten, the Italian woman dishes out Cadbury's Eclair Pops to queues of infants in colour-coded smocks. They clap their hands, bow, and run off with their trophies held high. There are not enough Pops to go round, but the children swap licks without recrimination and without wiping their noses.

There is a discussion about the high crime rate in Soweto. Just yesterday, a Blackchain supermarket was robbed by two armed men. The supervisor of the kindergarten says it is because people do not have work. The Italian woman says there is no such thing as no work.

'You know what the problem is? A garden boy will ask fifteen rands, and I may afford to pay only ten. So why he not accept the ten? If you want, you will work.'

The infants gather before us in a restless knot, punctuating a song of praise with misfired claps and random Ring-O-Rosies. Many cannot sing because of the lollipops in their mouths.

'That long, brown building is a hostel for migrant labourers,' says Bushy, as the minibus kicks up dirt. 'You see those hundreds and hundreds of cars parked behind the Jabulani Police Station? Stolen. All stolen. There is the Soweto Fire Station. One fire station for two and a half million people. And it only has two engines.'

What is a shebeen? Bushy says the best way to answer the American woman's question would be to visit one, even though it is not officially on the itinerary. Perhaps Mr Godfrey Moloi will be at home.

There are several American cars parked outside the low white walls, but that is mainly because Mr Moloi also runs a fleet of taxis. As well as a video movie service for weddings and other social occasions.

His business interests are diverse, but his chief personal interest is Godfrey Moloi. Self-made legend, man about township, friend of the rich and famous, the Godfather, the Captain, the Boss of Soweto. Godfrey Moloi rolls up the garage door and welcomes us into his shebeen, where jukeboxes twitter and bottles of beer wallow in buckets of ice.

'Black is Beautiful', says the poster of the psychedelic nude on the wall behind the cold metal benches. Moloi is big, pot-bellied, gruffly jovial. He has many stories to tell, but perhaps we would prefer to buy a copy of his book, My Life (Volume One), R13,25, autographed. As it turns out, Moloi is used to unofficial visitors.

He leads us into his lounge, panelled and varnished like the cabin of a yacht, with a zebra skin pinned to the ceiling. On one wall, a watercolour portrait of the Captain. On another wall, the Moloi family crest: IN VINO VERITAS.

Awkwardly, politely, his offer of drinks is refused. We must get back to the city. This perplexes Godfrey Moloi.

'You know,' he says, 'we blacks are not like you whites. You live behind high walls and never see your neighbours. Over here, if I am brewing beer in my garden, my neighbour will always come by and say hello.'

Now we feel even more awkward, but Godfrey Moloi slaps his belly and roars with regal laughter. So do we, a little. We are invited to sign the visitors' book. Noticing a

German address, Moloi proudly proclaims his ability to say goodbye in German: 'Half a dozen.'

The German diplomat offers an understanding smile: 'No, you say, "Auf Wiedersehen".'

'Yes, I know. Half a dozen.'

On the way out of Soweto, in a narrow, untarred street lined with semi-detached shanties, a small black boy runs after the minibus shouting: 'Abehlungu!'

Bushy laughs to herself, and then she shares the joke. 'He was pointing at the abehlungu. The white people.'

But then we knew that already.

IT'S A JUNGLE OUT THERE

Standing at the reception desk of my semi-luxury hotel in Lima, Peru, under the slowly simmering gaze of the man with the Uzi on his hip, I carefully hand over my camera, my wristwatch, my passport, my traveller's cheques, and my 22-blade Swiss Knife with the magnifying glass and the plastic toothpick.

I have second thoughts about the knife, but the man behind the desk curls his lips and says I shouldn't take any chances. There are bad guys all over the place. He gives me a small, unmarked key, and I wonder for a moment whether it wouldn't be a good idea to put that in the safety deposit box as well.

Then again, what's the big deal? The last thing I am going to look like, in this part of the world, is one of those dumb Gringo tourists. I take a deep breath and stride across the marble lobby, past the man with the Uzi submachine gun and the awning over his eyes. And then, in my Bart

Simpson T-shirt, my Mickey Mouse baseball cap, and my Australian surfing-shorts, I flip-flop down the steps and disappear into the crowd. You can never be too careful around here.

Over breakfast this morning, the Lima Times told me that 16 men and women had been gunned down by an unidentified paramilitary group at a fund-raising chicken barbecue in downtown Lima, just around the corner from the police intelligence bureau.

In the upscale neighbourhood of San Isidro, the Tupac Amaru Revolutionary Movement had claimed responsibility for blowing up 20 Mercedes Benzes in a series of dynamite attacks on luxury car sales concessions. The national cholera epidemic was back with a vengeance, with 200 cases reported in Lima and Callao in the space of a month. And Peru had won the Junior Section of the Pan American badminton championships.

For the visitor to Peru, the land of the Incas, the Andes, and the Amazon jungle, it may seem unwise to wander around in this time of social and political turmoil. No problem. There are cops everywhere you look.

Policemen in blue with machine guns, policemen in olive-green with truncheons, policemen in brown on motorcycles. Policemen with plastic visors raised over their riot helmets, like knights about to charge into battle. Policemen with fists raised to their lips, shrieking warning signals on concealed whistles. Here comes one now.

I'm sitting on the edge of a fountain in the wide-open sanctuary of the Plaza San Martin, trying to pretend that I'm not observing and categorising sub-species of Peruvian law-enforcement officer. I look the other way as the policeman raises his truncheon. Phwee-weep!

A woman is washing her hair in the fountain. Some of the lather has gone into her eardrums, so the policeman jabs her in the side. She moves on, all soaped-up and nowhere to rinse. Across the road, a group of men lean against a building, waving pocket calculators and fistfuls of American Dollars in the air. Volkswagen Beetles, reincarnated as taxis, race fenderless and dented around the square, as blind to robots as they are deaf to whistles. Still, they're probably safer than Mercedes Benzes.

I go to the Gold Museum, set in a suburb of Lima where the walls are topped with razor-wire and men with submachine guns stand guard outside electric gates, and I realise why Peru is no longer one of the world's great gold-mining nations: the Incas used it all up. There is so much Imperial gilt and glitter, so much glistening sweat of the sun, that it is almost enough to take your attention away from the collection of pre-Incan earthenware drinking vessels, moulded in the shape of pre-Incan sexual organs.

But this is a Catholic country, so my next stop is the Museum of the Headquarters of the Spanish Inquisition, where people once came to help the clergy with their inquiries. The scent of confession clings to damp and blackened walls, and there is a tableau of waxen figures melting in agony as hooded monks transcribe their screams with peacock-feather quills. The sweetly smiling curator clicks his fingers and tries to think of an English word: it turns out to be 'asphyxiate'.

The wing of the plane dips, shaking me from sleep and pointing out an endless vista of jungle and river beneath a thin ceiling of mist. El Inferno Verde. The Green Hell. This is the first big surprise. The Peruvian Rain Forest, global oxygen factory, home to untold species of fauna and flora, is not disappearing before my eyes at the rate of a football field a second.

Hey, I paid 60 bucks for a Save the Rain Forest T-shirt in New York, where the lady from Greenpeace told me that's how quickly the loggers and the oil barons were mowing the place down. Maybe you have to be higher up to get the big picture.

But right now, here I am, dangling my hand in the Amazon, cutting a swathe against the muscle of the current, when a B-Movie image suddenly leaps up from the murk. Piranha!

For the next two and a half hours, all I see are giant anacondas, electric eels, boa constrictors, thrashing saw-toothed alligators. But when we are close enough to touch them, they always turn out to be the same thing. Bits and pieces of the Rain Forest, drifting slowly down-river.

We take the Yanamono River off-ramp from the Amazon, and cruise gently downstream on coffee-coloured water. The lodge is like a set for a B-movie about man-eating fish. Only not as luxurious. Wood, vine, and palm-leaf thatch, with no electricity, no running water, no windows, no locks on the door. Well, OK, there is running water.

Without a hint of thunder, the sky opens up and the floor of the jungle turns to steam, and the macaws in the treetops tuck their beaks into their feathers and brood. I languish in my white canvas hammock, like a banana inside a peel, watching the silvery fringes of rain falling from the rooftop.

The toucan comes hopping down the walkway, with its beak-to-body ratio of 3:1, cocking its head to get a view past its own over-balanced proboscis. Beyond, all around, towering trees reach out with tangled roots and branches to reclaim their territory from the tourists. It's a jungle out there.

Dirty water glugging down a plughole. A rusty nail being prised from a plank. A neon filament humming and fizzing into light. The shrill chorus of a push-button telephone. Far away from home, in the depths of the emerald forest, the birds and insects make noises like civilisation.

I rap my knuckles against the buttress of a giant ceiba tree, protruding like a flexed tendon into the foilage. Ants emerge in confusion, transmitting frantic signals of crisis in the microcosm. The tree is alive.

My jungle-guide, an Amazonian Indian named Segundo Inuma, pulls on a plaited cord of vine hanging down from the tree-tops, and for a moment, he looks like a bell-ringer in a cathedral. 'You like to swing?'

The forest is a blur of bark, moss, chlorophyll and spider-web, as I tick-tock like a pendulum beneath the tall, creaking tree. An electric-blue butterfly darts out of the way. I choose a bed of leaves and I let go. There is no soil here. Just dead leaves upon dead leaves, waiting to turn to compost. In the distance, a slow, cracking sound. What's that? Segundo raises his palm and brings it crashing down. A tree falling in the forest. Happens all the time.

I catch a flash of red and yellow plumage in a shaft of filtered sunlight, but Segundo is staring at something on the ground. Quick as a chameleon, he pounces. Now he is shaking his fist from side to side, as if he is about to roll the dice. He lays out a big leaf, and opens his hand. 'Look. Poison-arrow tree frog. Very beautiful.'

Momentarily frozen, the frog is glossy red with black polka-dots. It's about as big as your thumbnail. Segundo looks around, biting his lip and frowning. 'You don't maybe have a box of matches in your pocket?' Hell, no. Thought you weren't supposed to smoke in the forest. But Segundo doesn't want to smoke. He wants to take the matches out, put the frog in, and send it airmail to a scientist he knows in Chicago. 'Good specimen.' But the moment is gone. The frog unfreezes, and with one red leap, disappears into the microcosm.

The sun sinks like a lead weight. Down by the jetty, Segundo is scooping water from a cedar-bark canoe. We are paddling on the Yanamono. It is like gliding on black ink. Green sparks of electricity from fireflies on the bank. The busy click-click of katydids. The beam of the Maglight falls on a startled white heron, and sweeps across to the unblinking eye of a giant owl on the opposite bank. But it's just an illusion painted on the wings of a butterfly.

In a treetrunk high above, a porcupine nudges its young back into the bark. A red-lipped frog clings to a reed. I turn around, and in a flash of jungle lightning, I think I see a piece of driftwood scything through the water. Probably just an anaconda.

The next day, with rain falling softly through holes in the canopy, we trek to a clearing occupied by the most fearsome tribe of blowgun-hunters in the Peruvian Amazon. Only a few decades ago, the Yagua were renowned for their cannibalism. These days, they're into Eco-tourism.

As we step into the clearing, the Yagua chief emerges from a big round hut, wearing an ankle-length grass skirt and red vegetable dye on his strong-boned face. He reaches for his blowgun. He puts it to his lips, sucks in his cheeks, and stabs a pack of Camel fastened to a tree 30 metres away. Then he hands the weapon to me.

It is not a pipe of peace. It is as tall and heavy as a bazooka, and it tastes of the jungle. The barrel dips low as I

'She's yours for only 50 poison-arrow blowpipes and a
piranha-tooth necklace.'

suck in my cheeks. Phhht. Not bad. A couple of millimetres to the left, and I would have hit my big toe. The Yagua chief laughs. Now we can do business. Because he wants to preserve his culture, he will not accept money for two small blowguns, one wooden carving, one necklace of catfish fins, and one piranha jaw with teeth intact.

But he will accept a carton of Marlboro and two 'I Love New York' T-shirts with glitter finish. Because I do not smoke or wear T-shirts with glitter finish, I do not feel that I have imposed my Western values on a Rain Forest Indian. I feel like an Eco-Tourist.

I raise my hand in the universal signal for 'Nice doing business with you', and I catch a glimpse of a Yagua woman emerging from a hut. Instinctively, she cups her bare breasts with her hands and retreats into the darkness. When she comes out again, she is wearing a Brooklyn Dodgers T-shirt.

In the lurching, rickety bus to Iquitos Airport, the man across the aisle catches me staring at the dark brown shape weighing down his right jacket pocket. He reaches inside, and the shape opens sleepy brown eyes. Baby spider-monkey.

As we round the corner, the man thrusts the monkey into my arms. The monkey holds on tight, liquorice-thin tail curled around the silver railing of the seat in front. Then, as an Eco-Tourist pops the flash on an Instamatic camera, the monkey pulls back its lips and screams. Everyone laughs. It is the sound of trees splintering in the forest.

From Cuzco to Machu Picchu, from the ancient capital of the Inca Empire to the Lost City of the Incas, is a distance of 113 km by rail. The journey takes three and a half hours. It's a slow train. There are steep gradients and switchbacks, and the tracks cut through villages where small kids and animals wait all day for the chance to chase the train.

The air is thin here, and as the train chugs along the Sacred Valley of the Urubamba River, average altitude 3 500 metres, its whistle begins to sound like the wheeze of air escaping from a tightly pinched balloon. It would be easy, at some point on this journey, for a person to board this train with no intention of sharing in the communal spirit of pilgrimage. No problem. Up front is a guy with an AK-47, and he doesn't look worried.

Like Stonehenge, Loch Ness, and the Bermuda Triangle, Machu Picchu is a place that brings out the mystic in people. We aren't even halfway there yet, and the woman two rows down is already talking about interplanetary alignment and the power of crystal meditation. I look out the window. There is the real world.

The green-white waters of the Urubamba, surging to pay tribute to the Amazon. The snow-capped peaks of the Andes, where the glacial trickle is born. Steam rising from thermal pools on the Andean plain. Bronzed kids skinny-dipping. A woman in a bowler hat, a shawl, and seven layers of petticoat leading a flock of llamas to pasture. Wind-whipped dogs fighting over a big yellow bone tossed from the train. A message in red on a crumbling farmhouse wall: YANKEE GO HOME. It is the end of the line.

The bus struggles in first up the snaking Inca pathway, and the view of the Sacred Valley gets more terrifying with every hairpin turn. At last, we get out and walk. Under threat of raincloud, the dark green peak of Machu Picchu rises above the ruined citadel, a scattered floorplan of palaces and townhouses and sacrificial temples.

No one really knows for sure why the ancient Incas felt compelled to build a city in thin air, on a forested clifftop 300 metres above the ground, with terraces and stairways gouged into the granite in places where only condors would dare to build their nests. But today, as the bus grits its teeth and lurches into second on a hairpin curve overlooking the brink of catastrophe, the theory that comes to mind is pilgrimage. The schlepp is good for the soul. And there is the view.

I sit on an ancient rock and contemplate the crumbling floorplan of the once-lost city of Machu Picchu, where a llama now nibbles on green green grass, framed through a stone doorway against the dizzying sweep of the Urubamba Valley. And as the clouds wrap themselves around the brooding peak, and the rain of the jungle begins to fall, I think to myself: Hey, what's the big deal? Sol Kerzner could have built this place in a day.

FOUR GOOD REASONS TO GO TO LIVERPOOL

I was only in Liverpool for a day, and there were two things I wanted to do, because I had come as a pilgrim. Firstly, I wanted to take a ferry across the Mersey, just like in the song by Gerry and the Pacemakers. Secondly, I wanted to go on the Magical Mystery Tour of Beatle landmarks and places of interest, leaving from outside the Lime Street railway station at 3 pm.

Along with all the other Beatle-fans waiting in the queue, I was childishly thrilled at the prospect of finally confronting the geographical reality of Penny Lane, and Strawberry Fields, and maybe even the churchyard where Eleanor Rigby was buried along with her name. So I bought myself a Beatles Tour Guide and Pocket Map for one Pound, booked a ticket to ride (four Pounds) and wandered down to the waterfront to fulfil the primary obligation of my pilgrimage.

'Life goes on day after day, hearts torn in every way, so ferry, cross the Mersey, 'cause this land's the land I love, and here I'll stay . . .' I sat on the top deck of the ferry, and the words echoed through my mind as the hovering seagulls squawked and soot from the funnel darkened the already sombre sky. On the banks, the city of Liverpool laboured under its ingrained coating of Victorian rust and grime, and even the solid brick bulk of the Anglican Cathedral looked more like a prison than a place of worship.

But beneath the grime there was grit, and beneath the grit there was a spirit of lust for life that found its ultimate expression (yeah yeah yeah) in the music and the mayhem of Beatlemania. Despite the enormous commercial potential of the Beatles cult, Liverpool's attitude to its four most famous commodities is clouded by ambivalence. On the one hand, the city appears proud of the way the Beatles conquered the world without sacrificing the gritty wit and integrity of their Scouse roots. On the other hand, it seems, they were just four more bored and itchy lads who couldn't wait to leave the place.

There are no municipal monuments to the martyred John Lennon, let alone any of the lesser Beatles, and it was only the twentieth anniversary of Beatlemania that galvanised the city council into sanctioning official Beatle bus tours. Street signs still point the way to the Liverpool Beatles Museum, but there is no such place, the entire contents having been sold lock, stock, and Beatle to an American millionaire before it was even opened to the public. Of course, there is always Mathew Street, the celebrated thoroughfare of record shops and coffee bars and the Cavern nightclub, where the resident fire hazard in the early Sixties was a band called The Beatles.

But the Cavern was demolished in 1973, to make way for a railway tunnel ventilation shaft, and the reconstruction is a poor substitute for the disappointed pilgrim. There is a melancholy air of reconstituted nostalgia about Mathew Street, with its motley selection of monuments ranging from the pedestrian (a multimillion Pound shopping mall developed in honour of the Beatles by a life insurance company) to the mundane (a cast-iron statue of a dull woman, ostensibly based on Eleanor Rigby) to the macabre (a bronze wall-sculpture of a shrouded figure that would look more at home in a medieval sarcophagus).

But somewhere along Mathew Street, affixed to the wall of a music shop, there is one monument that comes close to capturing the true spirit and significance of these four lads who shook the world. It is a simple historical plaque, and it says: John Lennon urinated here 27 times. Thanks, John.

'Do any of you have a favourite Beatle?' asked our registered Beatle tour guide, a stout, matronly woman named Hilary Oxlade, as the bus revved its engine in readiness. Aside from some isolated coughing and shuffling, the ice-breaking question was met with silence. One does not openly confess one's Beatle preferences beyond the age of 11, and anyway, most of the people on the bus were Japanese. Personally, I always thought George was the most outstanding Beatle, because you could never tell what he was really thinking underneath his smile. And he played the lead guitar, whereas John only played rhythm.

'Oooooooooooh, I need your loving, yes you know I do,' crackled the single speaker at the front of the bus as Hilary

Oxlade urged us to consider the statue of a nude man on top of the entrance to Lewis's Department Store. This was not, as I feared, another bizarre tribute to the memory of John Lennon. It was merely 'Exceedingly Bare', the Jacob Epstein artwork below which Lennon would arrange to meet Cynthia Twist at the end of her shift behind the shop counter. 'Hold me, love me, hold me, love me, oooooooooh, I ain't got nothing but love, babe ...' The bus slowed down outside number 64 Mount Pleasant Street, now a dingy yellow building, but once the site of the registry office where John Lennon, Beatle, married Cynthia Twist, several weeks pregnant.

On our left, the Liverpool Philharmonic Hall, where the Beatles never performed. 'But they did, we believe, attend several annual prizegivings here during their school careers.' On our right, the Crack, where the Beatles boozed before they became the Beatles. 'Only the landlord won't admit it, because they would have been under the legal drinking age in those days.' Straight ahead, the Liverpool Polytechnic, where John Lennon studied art and insubordination. 'It's just an empty shell now, but Paul is getting some money together to have it restored.'

The bus hissed to a halt outside the Empress Pub, in an area known as the Dingle, and we hopped off not for a pint, but for a peek at the little tenement house across the courtyard where Ringo was born to be a Beatle. It was a neat, bright house, now if not then, and Hilary Oxlade asked us nicely not to knock on the door or windows, because people were still living there. A baby doll peered from behind lace curtains in the upstairs window, and a kid on a tricycle whizzed by as we snapped pictures of each other standing in front of number 9 Madryn Street, Liverpool, England.

Since she looked old enough to be the mother of a Beatle, I took the opportunity to ask Hilary Oxlade if she had ever met the Beatles, and which one was her favourite. She shook her head with a smile of sweet regret. 'Lived in Liverpool all my life, but never met them.' Then she added: 'But I was working as an admissions clerk in the Sefton General Hospital, when Cynthia Lennon came in to have her baby. Only I wasn't on duty that day, I don't think.' The father of the baby, as it turned out, had always been her favourite Beatle.

Had this tour been conducted in the Sixties, we would probably have hailed every mundane detail in the domestic tapestry of Beatle-life with a fit of screaming and fainting. But now we were reverent, lost in thought, staring out of the window at an unfolding panorama of everyday suburban banality. The lollipop man with his white coat and peaked cap, smiling at the children as they ran across the zebra crossing. The ruddy-cheeked schoolboys with their skew ties and off-the-shoulder satchels. The couple kissing in the park. The lone baby sunning itself in the pram in the tiny front garden. The old man taking the old dog for a walk. You could probably write a song about all this, but it was already blaring out of the tape recorder.

'Down beneath the blue suburban skies, I sit and meanwhile back . . .' At first sight, Penny Lane looked nothing like the song. It was a bustling high street roundabout, not a cobbled Victorian alleyway, and the shops on either side clashed with the melody's swirling images. Posh Dog Canine Salon. Bredski's Kosher Deli. Jumbo Super Kitchen. The World Famous Penny Lane Winebar. Then, slowly, amidst the rush of traffic and shoppers, things began to fall into place.

There was 'the shelter in the middle of the roundabout'. There was the bank where 'the banker never wears a mac in the pouring rain'. And there was 'the barber showing photographs of every head he's had the pleasure to know'. (In particular, the heads of John, Paul, George, and Ringo.) The song was writing itself before my very eyes, but there was one thing missing from the picture. Nowhere was there a street sign confirming that this was indeed Penny Lane. Hilary Oxlade provided the answer. Over the years, every Penny Lane sign in the neighbourhood had been stolen by a gang of desperate Beatlemaniacs. What's worse, they had beaten me to it.

No one really expected Strawberry Fields to look like the song: 'Nothing is real, and nothing to get hung about... Strawberry Fields forever.' Still, there was an air of gloomy unreality hanging over the red wrought-iron gates of the Strawberry Field Children's Home. Layers of illegible graffiti covered the pyramid-topped gateposts, and there was a thick carpet of autumn leaves all the way up the driveway. It was a forlorn place, stuck in the middle of nowhere, shrouded in myth and legend because one man had floated over its gates in a dream of childhood. Or maybe, a nightmare.

The tape recorder played Imagine as we passed the exact spot where John Lennon's mother, Julia, was knocked over by a car, and then we pulled up outside a house in the leafy middle-class neighbourhood of Menlove Avenue. OFFICIAL NOTICE. PRIVATE. NO ADMISSION. It was a solid double-storey with stained-glass windows and a neat rose-garden, but it was clear that the present inhabitant had become a little fed up with his house being treated as a shrine by total strangers. So we kept a safe distance, and tried to imagine the boyhood John Lennon, sitting behind the upstairs window, writing silly poems and learning to play the guitar.

For a moment, I began to see the point of those Liverpudlians who had their reservations about turning the city into a secular equivalent of Bethlehem. There is, after all, more to the place than John, Paul, George, and Ringo. Likewise, there is more to the Beatles than Liverpool. But if you want to get a grip on the legend, there is no better place on earth to start. Yeah yeah yeah.

LAND OF MILK AND DECAFF HONEY

Within days of arriving in the US of A, I had already learned to speak American like a native. 'Hi, how ya doin',' the waitress would say, wiping the tabletop, chewing gum, and pulling a pen from her hair at the same time.

'Tuna submarine on sourdough,' I would reply, 'hold the mayo, extra pickles, and a decaff with half-and-half. Got any freshly-squeezed O-Jay? OK, and a blueberry muffin with peach and apple jelly on the side.'

After breakfast, I would carefully scan the colour-coded weather map on the back page of USA Today, a newspaper with roughly the same nutritional content as a blueberry muffin with peach and apple jelly on the side. It was October, the Halloween season, and the spectrum would range from the freezing white of Buffalo, to the chilly blue of Chicago, to the pumpkin-orange and fire-engine red of sweltering Miami and hot-as-hell Las Vegas.

I glanced at the front page. 'Halloween Scare Sweeps Campuses'. Centuries ago, according to the legend, the French seer Nostradamus predicted that a crazy killer would run riot on an American college campus on the night before Halloween. 'It's pretty scary,' said an American college kid. 'I'm moving out just in case.'

I gulped my decaff and asked for the bill. Sorry, the check. Then, like the couple in the Simon and Garfunkel song, I went out to look for America, guided only by my Delta Airlines standby pass and the icons of my American dreams. Mickey Mouse, King Kong, Clint Eastwood, Davy Crockett: I wanted to see them all, if not in person, then at least in the spirit of the land they made big.

With my nose pressed against the plate-glass, I looked down on the New World from the 110th floor of the World Trade Centre, where King Kong clambered with Jessica Lange in the remake. I took the lift. Elevator. In the days before Columbus, Manhattan was probably just another boring little island covered with trees and overrun by half-dressed aborigines who were neither Red nor Indian. Then came the immigrants.

Liberty's torch was just a candlewick from up here, and helicopters buzzed her crown like dragonflies. The Chrysler Building, colour of molten mercury, Gothic-spired, guarded by predatory gargoyles, was a poem as lovely as a skyscraper. And there was the old Empire State. You could paw your way to the observation deck on the 102nd floor and get a view of the city, but you wouldn't get to see the Empire State Building.

There are no skyscrapers in Washington, DC, capital of the nation. The tallest object around here is a stark white needle called The Monument, and it isn't even tall enough to dent the ozone layer. Nevertheless, there are some very tall people in this town. I stood outside the prison bars and stared at the White House, a wedding-cake of a mansion where the upwardly mobile come home to roost.

Across the road, a man had built himself a cage of sharpened bamboo spikes. He sat huddled in the corner beneath a sign that read 'Mr President, Free the POWs in Laos and Cambodia. A National Disgrace'. At least he had a place to stay. This was the day of the Great Homeless March, and hordes of people with no fixed abode had come to tell the President that they were mad as hell and weren't going to take it any more.

'We comin', we comin', we comin' . . .' But the President wasn't in right now. He was at Camp David, recuperating from minor surgery on the middle finger of his right hand. On television, a reporter asked the President to display the wounded digit to the nation. He just smiled and shook his head.

I followed the marchers from the Monument to the Capitol, counting spelling mistakes on placards. 'STAND TOGEATHER NOW.' 'ONE STELTH BOMER COULD FEED A MILLION HOMELESS.' A man rattled a king-size Coca-Cola cup under my nose. He was wearing a photo-ID card that identified him as Homeless Person. 'Hey, mister,' he said, 'you ain't maybe got a hundred thousand dollars to spare?'

Up the dazzling white steps, through two metal detectors, under the echoing dome, and into the public gallery of the Senate Chamber, where a sign warned: 'No expressions of Emotion Allowed'. For half an hour, expressionless, emotionless, I watched the Representative for Massachusetts, Senator Edward Moore Kennedy, shuffling papers, sipping iced water, and adjusting the knot on his necktie. Then I went to Disneyworld to meet Mickey Mouse in person.

There may be other reasons to go to Orlando — the international headquarters of Tupperware is just up the road — but I had come, like everyone else, to follow the Sign of the Spherical Ears. They're everywhere. Disneyworld, incorporating the Magic Kingdom, EPCOT Centre and the MGM-Studios Theme Park, is sixty times bigger than the principality of Monaco, although, to be fair, it is only two-thirds the size of Soweto.

Nevertheless, all 62 square kilometres of the Disneyworld Industrial Complex are so spick, so span, that they seem untouched by human hands. Even the rodents wear gloves.

What else do you want to know? Disneyworld is super-sensational with a capital $, and if you visit the World Showcase at EPCOT Centre, you can experience the sights, sounds and shopping malls of ten exotic destinations, without having to deal with muggers, foreign exchange, political instability, or funny toilets. Personally, I'd rather be in New Orleans.

New Orleans, on the sultry, steamy banks of the Mississippi River, is Disneyworld for grown-ups. In the French Quarter, where even the streets sound like they've had a little too much to drink — Bourbon, Burgundy, Basin, Toulouse — a girl walked by me and, for no apparent reason, lifted her T-shirt to reveal that she was wearing nothing underneath. And it wasn't even Mardi Gras.

The only thing coming to town was a tropical storm named Jerry, blowing in from the coast of Texas and hoping to be upgraded to a hurricane. In the supermarkets and Seven-Elevens, people were following the advice of civil defence authorities and stocking up on bottled water. Out on the streets, they were simply downing hurricanes. A hurricane, when it isn't named Jerry, is a blood-red rum cocktail, sold in polystyrene cups and drunk on the streets.

A clarinet squeals; a snare drum taps out a jazz tattoo. Ragtime. The humidity is 93 per cent, and the sky is the colour of unpolished chrome. Tomorrow, New Orleans could be Gone With the Wind. In the mean time, we hop aboard a streetcar named Cemeteries — the one named Desire runs in the opposite direction — and we head for one of the most popular tourist attractions in the city of New Orleans. The cemeteries.

On the banks of Old Man River, in the line of floods, hurricanes, and the seeping swamps of the Louisiana Bayou, the citizens of New Orleans have to contend not only with hell, but high water. This applies even when the carnival is over.

'The water table round these parts is so high,' said the ranger from the National Parks Service, 'that you'd have to begin bailing out before you even got your coffin in the ground. They used to try drilling holes in the bottom of the coffins and weighing them down with bricks. Didn't work. They'd just come rising back up to the surface. That's why we say you can't keep a good man down in New Orleans.'

We are in the grounds of the St Louis Cemetery, on the grimier fringes of the French Quarter, where good men and bad are not buried, but bolted in tombs as ornate as Italian mansions. Some women, too. Here is the tomb everyone has come to see. Marie Laveau, Voodoo Queen of New Orleans. On the face of the tomb, in rich red Mississippi mudbrick, Xs etched in supplication to the power of Gris-Gris. Voodoo magic.

'You come here at night, you make your X, you knock three times, and you ask Marie Laveau for a favour,' said the ranger. 'You leave a little something out of gratitude, and if your favour is granted, you come back and circle the X.' At the base of the tomb, I saw coins, a whisky bottle, beads, ear-rings. And higher up, several circled Xs.

As it turned out, tropical storm Jerry was just a lot of hot air, but one item from the weather reports stuck in my mind. Texas has a coastline. Somehow, under the spell of all those cowboy movies, I had always figured the place to be bone-dry and landlocked. I checked the map. Yup. Texas had a coastline. From Corpus Christi to Padre Island to Galveston on the Gulf of Mexico, there was enough rolling surf and golden sand to make California look stupid. Well, maybe next time.

Right now, I was standing in the middle of Dallas, Texas, wondering why I was the only guy in town. Glass skyscrapers, quartz, gold, black as oil, glinted in the noonday sun and admired their reflection in other glass skyscrapers. Every now and then, a stretch Cadillac with tinted windows and a boomerang-shaped aerial on the trunk would glide down the ghostly streets like a galleon. Otherwise, the place was deserted. Where was everybody?

It was only later, drifting through Dallas's air-conditioned, interconnected underground shopping malls and walkways, that I came to realise the simple answer. When it's high noon in Texas, only mad dogs and tourists go for a stroll in the sun. For this reason, I was not the only person loitering at the corner of Elm and Houston at about 12.30 pm.

This was the time, and this was the place, where a black Lincoln Continental cruised around the corner and headed for the freeway underpass on November 22, 1963. I hid behind the picket fence on the grassy knoll and carefully

*'What? You mean this isn't the official tour of
Paul Simon's residence?'*

followed the trajectory of the first car to come down Elm. Any place else, I would have been arrested for suspicious behaviour. Here in Dallas, it's called research.

I moved up to the sixth floor of the Dallas County Administration Building, formerly known as the Texas School Book Depository. I stood next to the window where Lee Harvey Oswald stood — forget JFK for a moment — and watched as a silver Chrysler swept serenely into the dip. It seemed to take forever.

Graceland, Memphis, Tennessee. I did not bump into the ghost of Elvis Presley, but I did get touched on the shoulder by a man in a dark blue uniform. 'Would ya come with me mister.' I stared into chrome sunglasses and felt All Shook Up.

In a small cubicle lined with control panels, blinking red lights and closed-circuit television monitors jump-cutting from room to room, I watched myself unzipping a camera bag, talking into a tape-recorder and scribbling furious notes. Suspicious Minds grilled me as Graceland flashed before my eyes. Somehow, I managed to convince the guys that I was not a spy from National Enquirer. They let me go.

Along with all the other pilgrims, I shuffled my way down Graceland's dimly lit corridors, taking care not to express inappropriate emotion as we passed the Hawaiian Room, the room where Elvis liked to watch four TVs at once, the display cabinet with the spangled kung fu suits, and the king-sized bed with the regulation wraparound safety belt in the jet called Lisa Marie. 'You are on camera throughout your visit,' said a pleasant female ghost voice, and I knew it was time to head for those wide open spaces.

By the time I got to Phoenix, Arizona, all I had to do was get a bus to Williams, Arizona, and then a steam-train to the south rim of the grandest hole in the ground known to man.

*If it's Tuesday, or any other day of the week, this must
be America*

As I stepped off the train, I saw a chalked sign that said: 'Winter storm warning today. Possible snow above 6500 feet.'

Don't let anyone tell you that the Grand Canyon is not a magnificent sight when it is blanketed by falling snow and drenched by rising fog. In fact, it is not any kind of sight at all. You could fall into it. I sat a little distance from the edge and waited while the weak sun cranked the weather out of the way. There it was.

The Grand Canyon is one of those sights that makes you wish you smoked Paul Revere. Then you could take a wild mustang down those chiselled trails, and barbecue a fish as the sun sank over the banks of the Colorado River. Or is it Marlboro?

I looked at the weather map on the back page of USA Today. The sun was shining orange in a place called Palm Springs. I went there. Forget Beverly Hills and Malibu Beach. Palm Springs, cradled by the San Jacinto Mountains in the Californian desert, is where the seriously famous come to unwind. The streets here are called Frank Sinatra Boulevard and Bob Hope Drive. Sonny Bono, for heaven's sake, is the mayor.

At the airport — 'The Palm Springs Regional Resortport' — they hand you a thick wad of discount vouchers, including $500 off your consultation with Dr Jane Norton, internationally known plastic surgeon. I hired a maroon Pontiac Grand Prix and cruised down Palm Canyon Drive, hoping to bump into somebody famous. But all I saw were infra-tanned blondes wearing leotards and bow-ties, date palms reaching for the sky and white Mercedes convertibles with personalised numberplates: 2BSWEET, GT2RUN and LCKY-ME.

In San Francisco, I wanted to get the best possible panorama of the Golden Gate Bridge, the Bay, the Victorian houses on the hill, and the anorexic Trans-America Pyramid, so I took a ferry to what used to be the most exclusive address in town. Alcatraz. These days, anyone can go there.

After years of criminal neglect and a brief period of symbolic occupation by a band of American Indians, the Rock where America's most wanted crooks came to brood is now open to innocent day-trippers. I wandered down the grim, echoing corridors, past the cages where Al Capone, 'Machine Gun' Kelly and the Birdman of Alcatraz had their wings clipped. I stopped at a tiny window in the communal dining-room.

There, beyond the bars, beyond the watchtowers, lay the Golden Gate and the city of San Francisco, just a life sentence and a ferry-ride away from the Rock. That sight must have been the cruellest punishment of all.

From sunny, wind-whipped San Francisco, I made my way to the north-western port of Seattle, where it was raining. But nobody seemed to mind. In the rain-slick streets, I saw the devil walking with his tail draped over his arm, and Mrs Marge Simpson, with her yellow face and blue beehive, running to catch a bus, and dracula, the werewolf, and a coven of witches waving at each other on their way to work. It was Halloween.

The front page of USA Today said something about a Chinese Honours student running wild with a gun on a college campus somewhere in America, but my eyes were already on the colours on the back page. Icy in Nebraska, warming up in Utah, getting colder in Colorado. Sun still shining: Florida, New Mexico, Nevada. All right, America. Maybe next time. Fill this up with decaff, will ya, honey?

TRUE
STORIES

WHAT I DID DURING THE STRUGGLE

On Sunday morning, when anyone in their right mind is too hungover to drink, let alone think, we gather at the commune in Yeoville for a drink and a think. The drink is muddy instant coffee with Cremora on top, served in chipped mugs that have not been washed for a very long time. But no one seems to mind, because the sticky brown residue serves to make a conscious statement. The commune does not have a maid. Either that, or she doesn't do mugs.

We think. About issues that concern every concerned young South African. About apartheid. About repression. About the State of Emergency. It is taken for granted that we are not the kind of people who take these things for granted. If we were not already concerned about these things, we would not be here this morning, drinking instant coffee and thinking about starting up our own alternative anti-government newspaper. OK. Business.

Very loosely, not wanting to appear too naively enthusiastic about the whole thing, not wanting to appear unnecessarily alert on a Sunday morning, we slouch towards the dining-room, cradling our coffee mugs like egg-and-spoon racers, and we sit down in no particular order of superiority and we have a meeting. About twelve of us have made it out of bed today, and one or two others have sent mumbled apologies. Besides our concern, we do not have much in common. Except maybe for our commitment. Some of us are law students, others are computer programmers.

There are some freelance writers, and a drama teacher, and a fine artist.

We have an idea about newspapers. 'I think we all agree that there is room for a newspaper that will really reflect the needs and aspirations of the community,' says the guy with the Sunday morning stubble and the fisherman's sweater, after we have all taken turns to tell everybody else our first names. 'Does anybody have any specific ideas?'

The girl with the Sunday morning stubble and the calico miniskirt says the newspaper should look something like the Weekly Mail, but should be more in touch with things at a grassroots level. Everyone agrees that the trouble with the Weekly Mail is that it is no longer able to see the grassroots for the treetops. It has published articles critical of the cultural boycott against South Africa, for instance, and has accepted advertisements from government departments. In any case, if the Weekly Mail is closed down by the government, somebody will have to plug the gap in the market.

'Look, I think there probably will be room for the Weekly Mail as well as us in the market,' says a guy in a Non-Aligned Summit T-shirt bought in Zimbabwe. 'We'll be offering people the other side of the story, basically. I mean, the Weekly Mail misses out on so much, it's just not true. Like, I know this guy who's active in BC, OK, and he says there's just so much happening on an organisational level in the townships, and you never read about that, OK, but . . .'

A law student grinds his Camel in a ceramic ashtray and interrupts. 'Yah but listen, we have to be quite careful about what we say about that kind of stuff, because we were checking the regulations out the other day, and they really are quite heavy.'

'Yah but surely that's exactly why it's so important to like get this newspaper together.'

'Yah I know but it's not going to be much use if they ban us after the first issue. It's just something we have to bear in mind from a legal standpoint. And also while we're on the subject, what I was wanting to know was what kind of standpoint will this newspaper be taking, I mean, what will its basic point of reference be?'

There is silence except for the scraping of a chair and the rat-like scuttling of a ginger cat as someone gets up to pour a second cup of instant coffee. Folding her legs beneath her on the sofa, the girl in the dress made from the white flour sack twirls her hair and shrugs: 'Aren't we going to be anti government?'

It is agreed that the newspaper should in essence devote its editorial energies to the struggle for a non-racial democratic South Africa, and should therefore strive to reflect the viewpoints of national democratic people's organisations with a broad base of community support. The fact that these organisations have been banned from fulfilling any function other than keeping their ledgers up to date places an even greater responsibility on . . . on . . . has anyone given any more thought to a name for the paper?

Brains storm, but there is no lightning. Someone suggests The People, but it is rejected on the grounds that people might confuse it with People magazine. This rejection is then rejected on the grounds that it is unlikely that People magazine is actually read by The People. Still, there could be problems with the copyright, from a legal standpoint. OK: The Struggle? The Voice? The New Voice? The Free Press? Opinion? Majority? Forward?

The guy in the fisherman's sweater is writing these names down on a clipboard. Some of them he marks with an asterisk, others he underlines twice, some he imprisons in inverted commas. Someone who is loudly trying to think of the Zulu word for Struggle stops suddenly when someone else says it is probably 'Inkatha'. OK. The name we can get back to. Does anyone know if that offer of a typesetting machine and desktop publishing set-up is still going? The guy who knows the guy from the South African Student Press Union says his friend is still on holiday, but he should be back by the end of next week.

Advertising. The guy thumbing tobacco into the bowl of his pipe says, yah, he got in touch with his contact at Hunt-Lascaris, and the guy reckoned they should come up with a dummy of the paper first, like a mock-up, and then tout it around so people could see what they were dealing with. Meanwhile, definitely, it looked like Shell Oil would be interested in taking a page in support of press freedom in the first issue.

'We should maybe be a little careful on that one. I read in the Weekly Mail that Shell were coming in for a lot of shit in Holland and England, that's why they're putting in all those ads.'

'Does anyone know who's behind those campaigns? Maybe we could try for an ad from them rather.'

The guy in the fisherman's sweater looks at his watch, and then at the ceiling, stretching his neck muscles to make the movement look aerobic rather than exasperated. When other people begin making aerobic movements, he stops stretching and asks whether anyone managed to write anything since last week. The ceiling needs painting. The drama teacher reaches into her canvas bag and says, here, this is that piece on the mime classes in Sebokeng. The piece is about eight pages of handwritten foolscap. 'Do you know if you need any kind of accreditation to get tickets from the Market? I wouldn't mind doing a couple of reviews.'

Next week on Sunday, if anyone can make it, we must talk about money. Coffee? White, please.

THE MAN WITH THE EMPTY GUN IN HIS HAND

In the lobby of the Great Hall of the University of the Witwatersrand, on the night the African National Congress came to town, there was a throng of people waiting to squeeze past the Beady Eye and the bored security guard. Things were starting to get a little claustrophobic, so I eased my way out of the bottleneck and wandered off to do a little shopping. The trestle-tables on either side of the door were loaded with T-shirts, tea-towels, books, sun-hats, posters, and paper pendants. Nelson Mandela was everywhere.

But it wasn't the wise, sprightly old sage we had come to recognise on national television, putting on his reading glasses to talk about nationalisation and the armed struggle. It was the young Mandela, the Scarlet Pimpernel, with his bold, defiant eyes and the dashing middle-parting in his hair. It was easy to see why this once-forbidden image was considered more viable, commercially and politically, than the real thing. It was a symbol. And symbols are not subject to change.

I couldn't decide between the T-shirt that said 'Viva Nelson Mandela' or the T-shirt that said 'The African National Congress Needs Your Support Now', so I bought a foam-rubber sun-visor in green, black, and gold, and I put it through the Beady Eye and sat down three rows from the front.

I took a look around the hall. Flags were waving, people were laughing. Almost every face was white. There was no sign of the evening's speakers, so I picked up the piece of paper on the floor and began studying the lyrics of the National Anthem. God Bless Africa.

When Walter Sisulu walked on to the stage of the Great Hall, the television spotlight gave his hair a frosted look, and he smiled as benignly as Santa Claus. Then he went over to the table and hugged Barbara Hogan, who had spent eight and a half years in jail for high treason. Sisulu had served 25. As they embraced freedom and each other, people stood up in waves, applauding.

Everybody seems to be hugging everybody else these days. It's good therapy, and some people need it more than others. That was why the ANC had called this meeting. It was a 'Call to Whites', the idea being to turn white fears into white hopes, or at least to persuade white South Africans to start thinking of themselves as South Africans rather than whites. Walter Sisulu stepped up to the podium, raised his right fist, and shouted: 'Amandla!' The answer roared back from a forest of waving fists, almost all of them white. 'Awethu!' Half the battle, it seemed, had already been won.

Then Walter Sisulu began reading from his notes. It was soothing. I took my comfort not from what he was saying, but from the revelation that an African National Congress politician on a platform is just as tranquillising as a National Party politician on a platform. It's the guys on the other side we have to watch out for: the orators.

Sisulu spoke, and Barbara Hogan spoke, and Popo Molefe of the United Democratic Front spoke. I found myself applauding things I wholeheartedly disagreed with, and from the sound of it, the feeling was infectious. Then, in the midst of the congregational chorus of 'Viva' and 'Amandla', I detected the bleat of a lone disbeliever. 'Praise God!' he was saying. 'Hallelujah!' 'Ay-men!' At first I thought he was being ironic, because he was making his interjections whenever anyone brought up the subject of white fears being justified, and the times we were living in being uncertain and dangerous. I turned around. The guy was definitely not being ironic.

He was slouching against the wall with his arms locked against his chest, and he was wearing denim jeans and a dark-blue cotton workshirt with the tail hanging out. There was a good reason for this, because underneath the shirt, in a holster on his hip, he was carrying a 9mm pistol. At last, the debate was starting to get interesting.

Very discreetly, two T-shirted marshals from the University of the Witwatersrand approached the man with the gun and asked him if he wouldn't mind leaving the hall. He didn't even look at them. He just shook his head. This was a call to whites, and he had come not only to answer it, but to reverse the charges. So they said he could stay, but would he please surrender his firearm. Now he looked them in the eye. 'No.'

He reached into his pocket and whipped out his Book of Life. 'This is my name, this is my number, this is my licence.' One of the guys jotted down the details in his notebook, but he was just playing for time. The hall erupted with applause, and I joined in, but only because I didn't want to make it obvious that I was eavesdropping on a crisis.

This was the real South Africa, up against the wall and shouting in whispers. 'Look. Will you please leave.' 'This is a public meeting, pal. You'll have to drag me out of here. And I can promise you one thing. I won't go alone.'

Where were the police when you needed them? Of course: they didn't attend political meetings any more. I toyed with the idea that the guy with the gun was actually a policeman, but then I saw something that convinced me otherwise. In one swift movement, in the middle of a three-man huddle, he reached for his gun, emptied the chamber, and handed the bullets to the marshal with the UDF T-shirt. They fell into his pocket with a click, and he smiled through pursed lips. Still, you do not silence a man because you take away his ammunition.

Up on the stage, Walter Sisulu was answering a question about the armed struggle. 'We are a peaceful organisation,' he said. 'We have only ever taken up arms to defend ourselves.' This was too much for the man with the empty gun. He shouted: 'Were you only defending yourself when the bomb went off in the Wimpy Bar?'

There were goose-like hisses from the audience, and a black man in a pin-striped suit, who had also been watching the pistol crisis with furtive interest, stood up and confronted the white man, nose to nose and seething. 'He couldn't defend himself, man! He was in jail!' There was some scattered applause, but most people, including myself (these guys were only a couple of centimetres away from me) were calling hysterically for calm.

The black man and the white man stared holes into each other, and their fists and their teeth were clenched in fury. 'Take out your gun,' said the black man, 'and I'll take out my gun, and we can shoot each other right here and now.' Then he marched away.

Some time later, between the closing of questions and the singing of the National Anthem, I saw the black man and the white man leaning against the wall, talking to each other in Afrikaans. They were not smiling; just having a conversation. The black man was talking about the history of the African National Congress, and why they had been forced to take up arms. The white guy was talking about Jesus.

I watched them talking to each other for a while, and they didn't seem to be coming any closer to consensus. But when the white guy walked out of the hall, I noticed something. He had forgotten to collect his bullets.

IS THERE A FIREMAN IN THE HOUSE?

I was sitting down to watch Rescue 911, the American television series about people trapped in real-life emergency situations, when I was struck by the funny feeling that I had forgotten something. Was it the salt? No, the salt was right there on the table in front of me. Was it the vinegar? No, the vinegar was in my hand, perched to sprinkle.

Was it the fork? The HP Sauce? The Ohlsson's Lager? I shrugged my shoulders. Everything I needed to demolish the heap of golden-fried chips in front of me, was in front of me. I began. Rescue 911, introduced by Captain Kirk of Star Trek, displayed its menu of mishaps and close-calls, many re-enacted by the actual participants.

There was a man who came home from work to surprise an intruder who shot him in the shoulder. There was a man who drove his Cadillac the wrong way down the freeway.

There was an old couple who stalled their station-wagon on a level crossing, just as a freight train came thundering down the tracks. Red lights and blue lights flashed as dispatchers alerted Emergency Services, and Captain Kirk announced a commercial break. Suddenly, I remembered.

I had forgotten to switch the stove off. Or had I? It was a long trek to the kitchen, and I didn't want to miss a single real-life emergency situation. On the other hand, I could probably use another Ohlsson's Lager. I grabbed a handful of chips and got up to check. The kitchen door was closed. Of course. I must have closed it after switching the stove off. I caught a glimpse of something alive and orange through the keyhole.

What was that smell? Potato chips? Sunflower oil? Electricity? OH, NO! I HAD FORGOTTEN TO SWITCH THE STOVE OFF! I threw open the door, ignoring the hiss of hot metal on the palm of my hand, and I made a cool, calm appraisal of the situation. HELP! HELP! HELP! KITCHEN BURNING DOWN! CURTAINS ON FIRE! BLUE SMOKE RISING FROM HOTPLATE! PAINT PEELING FROM CEILING! ELECTRICAL CABLES MELTING!

Memories of not paying attention during Emergency Drills at school and in the Army came flooding back to me, and a single recurring thought thrashed its way to the surface: 'Do not throw water on an electrical fire.' OK. I did not throw water. But it made no difference. The fire kept raging. I watched a tongue of flame lick open the plastic coating on a cable leading from the extractor fan, and I realised it was probably too late to switch the stove off now. Also, I decided not to bother about the beer.

I ran to phone the Fire Brigade, closing doors behind me — it was all coming back to me now — and barely pausing to watch the freight train crunching into the station-wagon. Where do you find 'Fire Brigade'? Fire Alarms & Extinguishers (Pty) Ltd, Firepro Security Services, Firestone SA, Firethorn Primary School, Fireworks Recording Studio . . . ah. I phoned the Fire Brigade and told them to come quickly because my house was on fire. I did not mention that I had forgotten to switch the stove off.

Then I ran to the kitchen, closing doors behind me, and I suddenly remembered: 'Use a BCF or Halon liquid-vapour extinguisher on a Class 1 fire.' I stood at the back door, watching the kitchen walls blister and blacken, breathing the acrid fumes of extra-roasted instant coffee and prematurely-caramelised white sugar, and I thought I had better do something, even as the red lights flashed and the klaxons clanged and the men in the PVC uniforms grabbed their axes and slid down poles.

I grabbed a bag of potatoes, slung it over my shoulder, and carried it outside. Then I rescued a sack of singed oranges. Then I grabbed a tea-towel and savaged a stray lick of fire heading for the dishwasher, and when the tea-towel burst into flame, I did what any level-headed person would do in the circumstances. I ran across the road and asked the neighbour if he had a BCF or Halon liquid-vapour extinguisher for Class 1 fires. He had two.

Seconds later, one of them was aimed at the heart of the fire, and as a fleck of dry foam wheezed from the nozzle, I realised why you needed two. The second one worked. Smothered in a bubble-bath of Bromochlorodifluoromethane — I checked the label just to make sure — the fire in my kitchen gasped its last, and all that was left was smoulder and devastation.

The Fire Brigade arrived. Several men held on to the end of a high-pressure hose, and as someone else ran to switch on the pump, I asked politely if they wouldn't mind checking inside first. 'Do you mind if we take a video for training purposes?' asked a fireman with a camera on his shoulder. 'Er, sure,' I nodded, thinking of Rescue 911.

The fireman emerged after a few minutes, and in the silent throbbing of the red light, I heard him say to his commanding officer: 'Ag, Sir, there's nothing to video here.' My face went fire-engine red, and I wondered if I shouldn't have thrown a little water on the flames after all.

The next day, when the insurance assessors and the electrical contractors had surveyed the damage, I rushed out and bought myself a big book called What To Do In An Emergency. I'm ready now. Come quicksand, come earthquake, come flood, come typhoon, come fallout, I'm going to get in that kitchen and make myself a nice big plate of chips. On second thoughts, maybe I'll just settle for the beer.

FOR A GOOD TIME, DIAL 1026

When I finally plucked up the courage to pick up the phone and call Amanda, the naughty housewife, she was engaged. The short, sharp beeps punctuated my heavy sigh of relief, and I held on until my pulse rate had returned to normal. I would try again later.

In the mean time, I ran my finger down the list of ladies in Classifieds, gliding past Candy and Sandy and Cindy and Angie, Lola and Lori and Sherri and . . . I stopped. 'Roses are red, violets are blue, Jacqui would love to fantasise with you.'

Jacqui. The name had a ring to it. I grabbed the phone, took a deep breath, and noticed that the cord connecting the handset to the casing was all tangled up. I hated that. I dangled the receiver in the air and let it slowly unwind, like a circus artist spinning by her teeth in the big top. Better.

With the dial-tone purring in my ear, I found Jacqui's number and hovered over the touch-pad. I touched. The last digit clicked through to exchange, and in the split-second before the electromagnetic signal pulsed through the coaxial cable to connect me to Jacqui, I slammed down the phone.

Maybe this wasn't such a good time to call. It was 3.22 pm. Who wants to fantasise at 3.22 pm? I called Amanda. What I liked about Amanda was her ad. 'Amanda the naughty housewife wants to tell all.' But when I dialled the number, all I could hear was the sound of Amanda telling it all to somebody else.

I made myself a cup of coffee, and I took the dog for a walk. At 5.52 pm, I called Jacqui. The phone rang. Four times. 'Hello,' sighed a voice, soft and American. 'How can I help you?'

I saw a swirl of heat and mist in a jacuzzi plunge-pool, and a lady with blonde, mossy hair talking to me on a pink plastic cellular phone. You know how it is. You can tell. 'Hello,' I said. 'Can I please speak to Jacqui?' The voice gasped.

'Oh dear. Jacqui's only here during the day. Can I help? This is Gina.' Gina? I hadn't even spoken a word to Jacqui, and already I was being tempted into infidelity. It just didn't feel right.

'It's OK,' I blurted. 'I'll try again tomorrow.' Sigh. 'Sure, honey. Bye now.' Click. I stared at the phone. A frisson of understanding shot through me, and I suddenly knew why people were prepared to pay R5,97 a minute to talk to a total stranger on the telephone.

It had nothing to do with sex. It was the novelty of getting good switchboard. I couldn't remember when I had last dialled a business number without some icy operator shouting 'Who's calling?' as I asked to be put through to someone who mysteriously wasn't there.

Then there were the crossed lines, the missed connections, the shrill interruptions and the canned xylophone melodies that stayed in your head all day. This was different. Sincere, friendly, eager to please, Gina seemed to have been waiting for my call all her life. It was like being in another country.

Amanda's phone rang. She answered. Suddenly, I was back in South Africa. There was a sharp edge to the voice, like steel wool on last night's dishes. In answer to my query, Amanda the naughty housewife said it would be R5,97 a minute, and we could talk about anything. 'Anything.'

She said the word in a way that seemed to narrow the possibilities down to one or two subjects. She said I could pay by credit card, and it would be reflected on my statement as Acme Hardware Company rather than Amanda the naughty housewife. I was pleased. It would look better on the IRP2.

Silence. Me and Amanda were ready for anything. But first: foreplay. 'Can I have your credit card number?' In loud, clear tones, I reeled off eight pairs of digits, pausing for Amanda to echo and verify.

'Expiry date? Master or Visa? Will you hold for me?' I held. In the background, I could hear the sound of a dot-matrix printer chattering to itself. Amanda came back and said three words. 'Talk to me.'

I gulped. What? Me, talk? I bounced a broad and simple question, hoping it would let me off the hook.

'Yes,' said Amanda, with the emotional intensity of a Post Office clerk franking postal-orders. 'I'm naughty. Very naughty. My husband's very rich. He's away on business for three out of every four weeks. He won't allow me to work. I live in this big house, and I've got all the money I need. But I get bored. Very bored. So people phone and talk to me, and sometimes, I phone them.'

What kind of people do you phone? 'Salesmen. I'm forever buying things.'

Amanda sketched a recent scenario. A travelling salesman comes to the door of her very big house. He's selling, maybe, vacuum cleaners. Amanda lets him in. She's wearing three items of clothing. Shoes, and a tight cocktail dress. The guy sits down on the couch. Amanda sits opposite him. He hauls out his product catalogue. She looks him straight in the eye.

'And then I uncross and cross my legs, and . . .' From what Amanda said next, I knew she had seen Basic Instinct. So I quickly changed the subject. 'Who do you think did it?'

Amanda cleared her throat and shifted gear, like a train going off the rails. 'I . . . I think it was the other lady. The psychiatrist.' Me too. But I wasn't about to spill my innermost feelings to a total stranger on the telephone. 'I think it was Sharon Stone.'

Well, that broke the ice. We talked. Movies, actors, actresses, you name it. 'Have you seen Final Analysis with Richard Gere?' asked Amanda. 'It's much better than Basic Instinct. But I can't stand Kim Basinger. She's just a dumb blonde.' I looked at my watch. It was a quarter past R29,85. I asked Amanda what she thought of South African men, not just travelling salesmen, but the whole bunch. Her voice grew cold.

'They're all pigs,' she said in my ear. 'You don't get honest men any more, I promise you. These guys around here, they're shallow. They just want to get into your panties. I like a man who can hold a conversation.'

My mind was on figures. Every second was costing me 0,0995 cents of money I hadn't even earned yet. I asked Amanda what she looked like, and I immediately felt like a South African man. But she answered anyway.

'I've got a white bikini on,' she said, 'because I've been lying by the pool. I've got long blonde hair. My own. Not from a bottle. I'm fair, medium height, nice legs, nice boobs...'

I was going to give Amanda my own identikit, based on Kevin Costner, but she went off the air for a second and came back saying, 'Anyway my dear, I must go now, there's people at the door. Will you phone again?'

'Of course,' I said, in my don't-call-me-I'll-call-you voice. Hmmm. I wondered, in the interests of cultural diversity, whether I shouldn't try talking to an American as well.

'A kitten of a gal. Sally the naughty Yankee. (Live!)' Switchboard put me through. Sally sounded sunburned and tigerish, as if she'd just been paged from the pool. But she was willing to talk. I knew the score by now, so I recited my number, and Sally went away. She came back. 'Sorry, honey. The machine won't accept your card.'

What! We went through the number again. One digit wrong. A 2 instead of a 3. Of course. Sally went away. This time, I heard the strains of non-specific jazz in the background. Then Sally. 'Gee, I'm real sorry, but it still won't accept. Of course I've got the right number. Maybe you have insufficient funds. If you like, you can deposit a bank-guaranteed cheque...'

Insufficient funds. I had heard some put-downs in my time, but this one took all the credit. Throwing caution and discretion to the phone-lines, I mumbled bye and punched in the number of the 'Exciting! Explicit! Totally Confidential!' service I had been avoiding so scrupulously until now.

Lucy answered. She had the kind of bright, chirpy telephone voice you hear when you've just won an all-expenses-paid holiday for two in a timeshare competition you didn't even know you'd entered. Lucy took my number and said we could talk about anything. Just like that.

'Actually, I'm new here,' she chirped. 'I've just come up from the Free State and I'm temping until I find a job. I'm really enjoying it. I love talking. People are so nice!'

I stared at the receiver in my hand. Did I have the wrong number? Did Lucy have the wrong number? I decided not to ask. Instead, for ten minutes, excitingly, explicitly, and totally confidentially, we talked about the Free State, the weather, the economy, switchboard operators, Leon Uris... almost anything.

'Ag,' said Lucy, just by the way, 'a lot of people who phone up are only interested in the dirty sex lines, but we try to keep things more open and friendly around here. If we can.' I had absolutely no problem with that, but I didn't want to go down in history as Lucy's least exciting caller. So I casually asked her what she did for fun. 'Oh,' she said, after a moment's thought, 'the crossword puzzle in Fair Lady.'

All right, that's it. No more subtleties, no more subterfuge, no more skirting around the issue. This time I'm going for the real thing. FIVE GORGEOUS GIRLS

WAITING TO DISCUSS THEIR WILDEST FANTASY OR YOURS.

'Hello,' I said. 'Could I please speak to one of your five gorgeous girls?' The gorgeous girl in admin said she would phone me back when she had authorisation, and then I could phone back and talk to whoever I wanted. About anything.

My phone rang. I rang back. 'This is Pin-Number D13,' I announced. 'Who would you like to talk to?' 'Um ... who is there?' 'Sasha, Pamela, Angelique ... ' 'Sasha.'

Sasha's voice was the sound of a stiletto heel crushing an ice-cube. I got straight to the point.

'My wildest fantasy,' I said, 'has always been to hear a gorgeous girl telling me her wildest fantasy on the telephone.' Silence. I could hear breathing, and it wasn't just my own. 'OK,' said Sasha, who had red hair, green eyes, hard, firm breasts, and long, slender, muscular legs. I know, because that's how she introduced herself.

'My wildest fantasy you might not like,' swooned Sasha, 'but it's mine, and you want to hear me relate it, OK?' OK. 'My wildest fantasy is basically that I'd be in a situation where ...'

Through a mixture of grim determination and politeness, I held on as Sasha detailed a wild fantasy involving a Brigitte Nielsen lookalike, a tall, very dark, and handsome man, a hotel room with wall-to-wall mirrors and a Do Not Disturb sign on the door, and, well, Sasha.

I didn't have to say anything. I could have put the receiver down and gone out to take the dog for a walk. But I held on, listening to Sasha take great gulps of air through her teeth, until, after what I hoped was not too much longer than R89,55, I heard her say: 'You call Sasha again, honey. OK?'

Well, maybe. I mean, there are still four other gorgeous girls out there. On the other hand, next time I'm looking for a good time on the telephone, I think I'm going to cut out the middleman and just dial 1026. Hey, you know, it's cheaper.

I'D WALK ON FIRE FOR A PORSCHE 911

Inside the lecture room of the Lincoln Country Lodge, the easy part of the course had come to an end. We had been through Anchoring, and Reframing, and Modelling. We had learned the Three Steps to Personal Power, the Seven Character Traits of a Champion, and the Five Keys to Wealth and Happiness. Now there was one more thing to do, and then we could go home.

It was nine o'clock on Saturday night. I took off my shoes and socks, rolled up my jeans, and looked out the window. The darkness was quiet and suffocating. But the fire was burning nicely. The logs were turning into coals, and sparks were shooting from the flames. I took a deep breath, clenched my fist, and filed outside with the rest of them.

Most of us were laughing. Firstly because we had actually paid good money — hell, R325 — to do what we were about to do. Secondly because we had no doubt that we were going to do it. And finally, because laughter is the body's natural endorphin for sheer terror.

Down by the logfire, a shallow bed had been dug in the dirt road leading to the bungalows. The area was about ten strides long by two strides wide, I reckoned. Suddenly, nobody was laughing. A guy in a boiler suit and a helmet with a perspex visor cautioned us to move out of the way. He was carrying a long-necked shovel heaped with hot coals. He spread the coals, patted them down, and went back for more. Soon the bed was glowing like a tongue of molten lava.

A soft drizzle was falling, but it turned to sizzle as soon as it hit the coals. We stood around staring at them, and it struck me that no matter how many times you have gathered round a braaivleis with a beer in your hand, or sat in a lounge gazing at a logfire, you do not ever appreciate the true nature of fire until you are about to walk over one, barefoot and stone-cold sober. Without getting burned.

When someone first told me this was possible, I did not want to know how. I wanted to know what for. I just got the feeling that there were better things to do on a Saturday night. Also, during my military training in Bloemfontein, me and about forty other guys used to share a bungalow with a pyromaniac. He used to sit on the edge of his bed and stick wads of cottonwool between his toes, the way girls do when they paint their nails. The difference here was that the wads had been soaked in methylated spirits.

Then, while the new guys stood around watching with wide-open mouths, he took out his Bic lighter and set his toes on fire. This always seemed to me to be a particularly desperate way of coping with National Service. It never really bothered me that the guy did not scream or fry. I just put it down to his thick skin, and his ignorance of the laws of nature. But now, away from the Army's independent universe of inverse logic, I began to wonder which one of us was really ignorant. What if . . .

So I signed up for the Personal Power Institute's Mind Revolution Seminar, incorporating The Firewalk Experience. What the hell. There wasn't that much to watch on television, anyway. I walked into the lecture room of the

Lincoln Country Lodge at about seven o'clock on a Friday night. The signs were not good. A tape deck was blaring a song called Sanbonani, by PJ Powers. 'What you gonna do, in a world without love? It could all come true, this could be a new age dawning, for the New South Africa.'

The walls were postered with the kind of pop psychology slogans you find in fortune cookies. REALITY IS A MYTH. BELIEF IN LIMITS CREATES LIMITED PEOPLE. THE MAP IS NOT THE TERRITORY. IF I CAN'T, I MUST. RAPPORT IS POWER.

But it was too late. I couldn't get cold feet now. I went up to the desk and got my name tag and a form to fill in. 'Don't forget to complete the indemnity on the back as well,' smiled a woman whose tag said Joy. Under the thatched roof, chairs had been arranged in a crescent around a movie screen, an overhead projector, a television monitor, and a couple of lecture boards.

People were sitting randomly in places, frowning and biting their ballpoint pens. Like me, they seemed to be having difficulty with a couple of the questions. What has your greatest achievement been to date? What do you aim to achieve in life? How would you know if this course had helped you attain your goals?

I recognised a guy standing next to an anatomical model of the human brain at the front of the room. He wore a business suit and a beard, and he looked like the kind of guy who knew the correct answers to the above questions. Now where had I seen him before? Oh yes. He was the guy on the cover of the Personal Power Institute's Mind Revolution Seminar invitation pamphlet. There was a picture of him with his trousers rolled up, tramping across the hot coals as if they were little black grapes. His eyes were lightly glazed, his mouth a little open, his stride as sure and direct as the little green man in the pedestrian robot.

'The firewalk,' explained the pamphlet, 'is a metaphor for possibilities. Neuro Linguistic Programming is not a mystical skill, but rather a practical set of tools on HOW to be able to get yourself to take EFFECTIVE ACTION in spite of any fear you might have. The road to success lies ahead of you. Winning starts with beginning. Take up the challenge NOW!'

That did it. The firewalk was only a metaphor! Mind over metaphor, feet over coals! It seemed so simple. The only thing I had to fear was fire itself. I hovered no longer. I signed the back of the form, indemnifying the Personal Power Institute against any claims resulting from any activity I might undertake during the course of the Mind Revolution Seminar.

Let the Revolution begin. There were about forty of us in the class. I was prepared for ordeal by fire. But nobody told me about ordeal by introduction. The guy with the beard introduced himself as Charles Bradfield, Neuro Linguistic Programming expert. A guy with black hair, glasses, and a wry, knowing smile introduced himself as David Assaizky, Bradfield's fellow expert and presenter. Then it was our turn.

'I'd like you all to get up now,' said Assaizky, 'and introduce yourself to three people in the room who you don't know.'

There was a scraping of chairs and a mass babble of embarrassment as we arose to swap inanities with our fellow initiates. It had been suggested that we find out what each other's zodiac signs were. I met a Scorpio and a Capricorn. None of us knew what kind of people we were supposed to be, which was a relief. I met another guy who stared at my name tag, held out his hand, and introduced himself as me. We were all a little nervous.

A brass schoolbell pealed, and we all sat down. But not for long. Starting with the guy nearest the door, we stood up in turn and announced our occupations, expectations, and motivations. As it turned out, the guy nearest the door had already been through all this. Including The Firewalk Experience. Besides an aura of steely self-confidence, he was wearing a white shirt with a thin black tie and black checked Oxford Bags. There was a gold dot on his name tag, which stood for Graduate.

I looked around the room. A lot of people were wearing gold dots. This worried me. Why would anyone need to undergo a Mind Revolution more than once? Why would anyone volunteer to walk on fire for a second time? I decided to put the question to the nearest Gold Dot at the earliest opportunity.

'I'm an import-export agent on the JSE,' said the guy with the tie. 'The last time I came on this course, I made myself a promise. I said I was going to earn enough money to buy myself a Sixteen Valve Golf GTI.'

He paused.

'It's parked outside.'

Everyone applauded, although the air was abuzz with the secret thought that there must be easier ways to finance a Golf GTI than walking on fire. Now, all fired up, the novices spoke.

'I'm a gold mine manager, and I'm willing to do anything to improve the price of gold.'

'I'm a professional rebirther, and I want to see if I can enrich my own life even more.'

'I've just come out of the Army, and I want to get myself ready for Civvie Street.'

'I used to be a commodity broker, now I'm a student. Basically, I think this sounds like a pretty good party trick.'

'I'm a psychologist. I want to find out who I am.'

'I'm still in school. I came with my father.'

'I'm a financial journalist. I'm here because I personally believe there's no difference between me and the President of the United States.'

'I'm in the bulletproof-vest business...'

'I work for AECI Explosives...'

Finally, a tall man with wavy silver hair arose and announced himself in a heavy Greek accent. 'I'm the hotel manager. I'm here because I'm not insured for damages, so I hope everything goes OK.'

Having successfully endured the who and the why, we began to get on with the how. And how. Split into pairs, we were handed lengths of nylon rope and instructed to tie ourselves together and escape without undoing the knots or otherwise cheating. This seemed to be a metaphor for filling in an income tax form. Many minutes later, when I was beginning to get the feeling that I was destined to spend the rest of my life linked to an Austrian timeshare resort developer, a Gold Dot came along and set us free. It was self-kickingly simple. A little bit of lateral thinking, a little bit of inside looping.

I said thank you and asked the question. What made you come on the course again? The Gold Dot, wearing that same glow of serene inner knowledge, looked at me and smiled. 'Have you ever walked on fire?'

I said no. 'Do you believe you're going to walk on fire?' Not really, but I said yes anyway. 'Then ask me that question again tomorrow night. Except you probably won't need to.'

Now I was really worried. There was an incense of rebirth about the whole thing. A phrase surfaced slowly from the swamp of cliché, and I heard it suddenly toll with meaning. Baptism by Fire. Of course, I had nothing against altering my basic state of consciousness. In fact, the more I thought about it, the more I thought it would be a good idea to change my mind and go home to watch television.

But my fears began to ease a little when David Assaizky spoke. He had a flip, laconic style, and there was something he said, something he kept repeating at the peaks of his discourse on the power of the mind, that made me think maybe everything was going to be OK after all. 'If it doesn't work for you, it's a lie.'

This became my mantra. I clung to it like a sandpaper raft in a sea of syrup. It was my defence against Sanbonani by PJ Powers, and my salvation on the many occasions when we had to split into groups and stare into each other's eyeballs, and beyond them into the antechambers of the mind itself. For me, this was the Big Truth about Neuro Linguistic Programming. It's a lie. I surrendered myself to it, and began to believe that I could do anything. Including walk on fire.

Neuro Linguistic Programming, when you first hear the term, sounds like an Orwellian euphemism for brainwashing. But it's closer to brainscrubbing, a practical process of stripping away layers of doubt, fear, and denial and replacing them with new layers of belief, power, and action. Well, that's the theory, anyway.

NLP has applications in business, psychology, education, and — pass the sandpaper — personal motivation. It's the

brainchild of two American academics, John Grinder, a Professor of Linguistics, and Richard Bandler, a Professor of Computer Programming. In essence, it's a way of getting through to the Right Hemisphere of the brain, the twilight zone beyond the grasp of logic and analysis and mathematics.

The Right brain is the domain of music and metaphor, sex and emotion, jigsaw puzzles and dreams. Somewhere in there lies the key to walking on fire. Logic says you're crazy, analysis says you'll get burned. Guess what: it's a lie.

In the lecture room, NLP is a bit of Dale Carnegie, a bit of Norman Vincent Peale, a bit of very superficial hypnotherapy. Much of it is grindingly familiar common sense packaged in fingerclicking pop psychology. 'You are the way you feel' becomes 'Your state is determined by your Internal Representations'. 'Think positively' becomes 'Motivate yourself by using Submodalities'. 'Count your blessings' becomes 'Reframe and scramble your content'.

There is no doctrine, no message, no cult. The big class question is not 'Who wants to be saved?' It is 'Who wants a Porsche Nine Eleven E?' OK, maybe there is a little bit of a cult. But the one thing NLP does have that all cults are supposed to have, is rituals.

'Hand buzz!' shouted Charles Bradfield at 10.30 pm, when he noticed that the class was getting a little restless in both hemispheres of brain and bum. We were getting used to this by now. We stirred from our seats, stretched and yawned, and came together in a rough circle. Then we bent down a little and waved our right hands, flexing the fingertips like electricity. At the peak of it all, we lifted and roared. 'Ahwharrrrrrghhhhhhhhhhhhoooooooowwwwwww!'

'Let's do it again,' said Bradfield. 'And this time, let's blow the thatch right off the roof.' A little voice cut nervously through the buzz. 'No, please, I don't think so.' It was the hotel manager.

Bradfield gave us the rules for tomorrow. No alcohol. No pantihose. (Nylon catches fire.) Don't forget to wear a jersey. And bring towels. To dry your feet at the end, because someone will be waiting with a hosepipe to wash away the bits of hot coal that get stuck between your toes.

At home at midnight, I did a little research. Not into NLP, which, as far as I was concerned, was merely a metaphor for firewalking. I found the subject catalogued between Voodoo and Water Divining in Mysteries of the Unexplained. Firewalking is an ancient art, routinely practised on holy days by Hindus in Durban, Navajos in America, and Orthodox pilgrims in Greece. Temperatures are usually around 1 200 degrees Centigrade — higher than the melting point of steel — and, with rare exceptions, the participants survive the experience without so much as a blister on their big toe.

Scientists who have studied the phenomenon from a safe distance tend to conclude that the firewalker is protected from burning by a layer of sweat that builds up on the soles of the feet. This is known as 'The Leidenfrost Effect'. But there is a problem with this theory, as anyone who has ever inadvertently stepped on a smouldering ash heap will confirm. Feet burn quicker than they can sweat.

So the favoured theory is simply 'Auto Hypnosis'. This may explain the connection between firewalking and the Golf Sixteen Valve GTI, but it is of little comfort when you are lying wide awake at 2 am, lucidly aware of the properties of fire, and the scientifically proven effect of hot coals on bare feet.

At lunch the next day, I was relieved to discover that I was not the only participant on the Mind Revolution Seminar to have undergone an overnight conversion to reality. Nodding grim agreement over dessert, we conceded that firewalking was a possible and valid thing to do. For other people. We ourselves, having more stubborn states of consciousness, were convinced that we were volunteering for the Third Degree. It was a cold fact: people, maybe just one in a hundred, got burned on these courses. Hence the indemnity.

'The thing that worries me,' said the professional rebirther, 'is that we've only got another seven hours to go before we do it, and those guys in there don't seem to be any closer to giving us the formula.'

After lunch, we did not get the formula. We watched videos. Sylvester Stallone winning the World Armwrestling Championship in Over the Top. Eddie Murphy posing as an irate customs inspector in Beverly Hills Cop. Rodney Dangerfield reciting Dylan Thomas in Back to School. Now, more than ever, I knew that I should have stayed at home and watched television.

We were learning Modelling. In NLP, the art of expanding your identity by copying someone else. If you want to run the Comrades, you model Bruce Fordyce. If you want to Rock 'n Roll, you model Bruce Springsteen. You need to believe, and you need to look and feel the part. 'Fake it till you make it.' Other than that, all you need is the formula.

Over supper, I looked around and wondered about the market for liquid asbestos foot spray. There had to be a formula somewhere. Nobody spoke about firewalking. The guy in the bulletproof-vest business said a client of his had been shot in the head after someone had tipped off the other side. It was terrible. The guy hadn't even paid for his vest yet.

It was 8 pm. Charles Bradfield said he hoped we were feeling scared. 'I'm feeling scared. You have to feel scared. You can't conquer fear if you don't feel it.' He reminded us that nobody was compelled to do the firewalk. 'But if you want to, you're helluva welcome.'

Nobody kept their shoes and socks on. For R325, you want to get your money's worth. On the carpet in the lecture room, we modelled the firewalk. It was easy. Take a deep breath, keep your feet flat, follow a straight line, don't run, don't look down. There was one more thing. The formula. Cool moss. That was it. You had to keep saying it to yourself, over and over, to silence the side of your brain that kept saying 'hot coals'.

Hot coals. Hot coals. Hot coals. The guy with the helmet was spooning them and spreading them, like caviar on toast. I stared at them. They glared back. In the pit of my stomach, I was gripped by a powerful mixture of blind terror and ecstatic abandon, the way I used to feel when I had to write a trigonometry exam at school. I never swotted, and I always knew I was going to get two per cent. But for some crazy reason, it made me feel high. It wasn't just adrenalin. It was . . . yes, of course. The sound of the Right brain laughing at the Left brain.

Cool moss. Cool moss. Cool moss. I stood on the edge, feeling the fire and chanting the formula along with everybody else. People were crossing at a brisk pace now, staring straight ahead, talking to themselves, striding like soldiers at a medal parade.

I fell in line. Fresh coals were shovelled on and raked over. There was the sound of wild whooping and laughter.

It seemed to come from the other side of the firewalk. I was about halfway down the queue. We moved forward. Cool moss. A girl stepped on to the coals, walked a little way, and then veered suddenly off course. She fell sobbing on to the wet grass. Hot coals. I watched the guy in front of me do it. I was transfixed by the petals of yellow flame that shot up from his heels as he crossed to the other side and punched his fist into the air.

Then I took a deep breath, stared straight ahead, and walked on fire. It was as easy as trigonometry. I don't remember much of it, except that it didn't feel like hot coals. Nor, for that matter, cool moss. It was more of a dry and brittle sensation, like walking on champagne corks. Towards the end, I seem to recall, my feet were beginning to convince my brain that I wasn't really walking on cool moss after all. But I didn't burn. I tingled for a while, and then I soared somewhere into the furthest regions of outer space, and I didn't come down until much later, when I had a couple of cold Castle Lagers in the Lincoln Country Lodge bar.

Now it is some weeks later, and I think I know the answer to the question. What for? Yes, it is true. My life has changed. I have discovered the meaning of PERSONAL POWER. I have developed a POSITIVE MENTAL ATTITUDE. I have learned to give DIRECTION to my dreams. I have modelled myself on Sylvester Stallone and Eddie Murphy. I have focused my energies on a Sony Compact Disc Player, and a ten-roomed townhouse on top of Northcliff Hill, and a metallic blue BMW with fuel injection and a sunroof.

What the hell. If it doesn't work out, I can always join the fire brigade.

SATURDAY NIGHT AT THE GARAGE

When you've just spent four and a half hours on a hot and crowded flight from a tropical island, with babies howling fore and aft, the last thing you want to worry about is the little red light flashing on the dashboard of the kombi that's ferrying you home. So who's worrying?

It's half past eleven on a Saturday night, and I'm sitting in the front seat, pretending not to notice that the driver hasn't noticed. We're still cruising. That's the main thing. The little red light, by tacit communion, is discreetly ignored. It'll go away. It's probably just a loose connection in the fusebox. At worst, a blown brake-light bulb. Maybe the boot-latch isn't properly secured.

Maybe... hmmm. Just what I thought. We're standing in the forecourt of the Shell Service Station, Eastgate Shopping Centre, staring at the shredded, melting remains of a black snake that must somehow have worked its way into the engine.

'Fanbelt,' says the driver. Of course. I knew that. Now all we need to get back on the road, and home before midnight, is a common-or-garden pair of pantihose, looped and knotted around wherever fanbelts are supposed to go before they slip off. It's at moments like this that life's really important lessons begin to drive themselves home.

One: You should always carry a spare fanbelt in the back of your car. Two: women, these days, don't wear pantihose. Three: If I'd caught the bus, I'd be fast asleep by now. I'm transfixed by the sight of murky water percolating in the radiator of a broken-down VW Kombi, when a Pavlovian impulse pops into my head. Coffee.

The guy on nightshift, under no obligation to take an interest in anyone else's problems, slips me change for a R5 note from behind his glass booth. You can't blame him. He probably spends half the night dispensing change for the phone, and the other half dispensing directions to jet-lagged tourists who can't find their way to Johannesburg from the airport. I push the button marked 'Coffee, White, No Sugar', and I watch a jet of steaming liquid gush from the udder into empty space.

'We're out of cups,' says Nightshift, refunding my money with a scowl. This is going to be one of those nights. In fifteen minutes from now, it's going to be one of those mornings. Never mind the bus. I should have caught the train. Here comes one now, clattering down the tracks under the heavy metal burden of its freight.

Just a second. We're nowhere near the railway line. I hang up on the AA's answering machine — 'Please be patient, all our operators are busy right now' — and suddenly, I begin to feel a little less desperate about our immediate situation. That is the sound of a wheel being driven over a field of furrowed speedbumps, cushioned only by the loose flap of what used to be a tyre. This guy's in trouble.

He scrapes on to the forecourt, stalls the engine, gets out, slams the door, and . . . hey, he's wearing a kilt. Here are his problems, in descending order of significance. He is a National Serviceman, attached to a Scottish infantry regiment. He had a blowout, left front tyre, about six kilometres back. He's got a spare. He doesn't have a jack. This is a military vehicle. It has to be back at base by midnight. It is now ten to twelve.

'Can I borrow your jack?' Of course. It's not as if the guy's asking for a fanbelt, or anything. Here come two more of life's little lessons. One: there is no elegant way to attempt to fix a blowout, when you are wearing a kilt. Two: VW Kombi jacks do not work on military vehicles. Don't ask why. Maybe it's got something to do with the fact that there is a dent the size of King Kong's fist on the passenger side of the car.

The guy in the kilt, red-faced, fair-haired, splodges of grease on his dress-shirt, is not having a good night. Come to think of it, he is probably not having a good year. 'This is it. This time . . . ' Clang of wheel-spanner, tyre-stains on tartan, anguished glance at watch. ' . . . they're going to court-martial me.'

Let's be reasonable. It's ten past twelve. The military vehicle has not turned into a pumpkin. There is no legitimate cause for panic. No, we haven't got another jack.

'Can't you just phone your base and tell them you've had a blowout?'

A look of uncomprehending exasperation. Obviously, we've never been in the Army. And if we have, we've never been in a Scottish infantry regiment. 'No. I can't. They won't believe me.' The naked rim of the left front wheel has not just been chewed by six kilometres of contact with the tarmac. It has been minced. Further in, the axle has been gently bent like a banana. Even if you could fit the spare on there, you'd only be able to drive in a right-handed circle. Round and round.

The guy in the kilt doesn't need to hear this. Of all the Samaritans at all the service stations in all the world, he had to run into us. We're pointing at the rim. We're shaking our heads. We're not taking this seriously. But there's still one chance. The man in the glass booth. The infantryman strides across the forecourt, pleats rustling in the midnight breeze.

If he thinks he's going to get a cup of coffee, he's in for a surprise. But he doesn't want coffee. He wants a jack. And he wants it now.

This is a service station, right? Right. Petrol, oil, water, 24 hours a day. Coffee, too, if you bring your own paper cup. But there's a limit to what you're going to get at 12.30 on a Sunday morning. Even if you shout. Even if you bang a fist on the counter. Even if you say: 'Look, I'm a National Serviceman! I've got to get back to camp! They're going to court-martial me! They're going to throw me in jail! All I'm asking is for you to get me a jack from inside the workshop! Do you understand?'

That's what the glass barrier is for. Service. If the guy on nightshift wasn't a petrol station attendant, he'd make a great customer relations clerk at the Department of Home Affairs. Except for one thing. He's actually doing something. He's picking up the telephone. Infantryman bangs both fists on the counter. He walks over to the callbox. Plan Z. He's going to call the AA.

Ten minutes later, he's still waiting to be connected to an operator — Saturday nights and Sunday mornings are peak times for blowouts and shredded fanbelts — when four armed men come strolling out of the shadows. This is it. Eastgate Security. It's like a scene from the Wild Bunch, except these guys are armed with knobkieries. Nightshift steps out of his booth. He points. Four sets of eyes swivel across to the callbox.

An agitated conversation in a variety of vernaculars. One man slowly unholsters his knobkierie. He begins slapping time against his palm. The guy in the kilt realises what's happening. At last! He hangs up on the AA and hurries

'I've told you already ... there's no Jack working here!'

over, pointing at his watch, pointing at his car, rapidly running out of courtesy and patience.

But he's got the wrong end of the knobkierie. These guys haven't come to help him find a jack. It's unbelievable: they're security guards, they're in uniform, and they're just going to stand by while that minibus over there pulls away. They're not going to order the guy to stop and hand over his jack. What's the matter with them?

The conversation gets louder, sharper, less polite. One security guard unleashes a weapon far more dangerous than a knobkierie: an index finger. 'Don't use vulgar words with me, boy.' That's Security talking to Infantry. There is a brief duel of index fingers, and then a car pulls up on the forecourt. It's for us: Good Samaritan, with fanbelt. But the tartan swirl gets there first. 'Can I borrow your jack?'

It fits! Hardly has the first wheelnut been prised off, when the speedbumps of Eastgate judder with the corrugated sound of tyres on fire. It's the South African Police. Screech, slam. There's a Cortina, a pick-up van, and enough policemen, plainclothes and uniform, to patrol a Provincial rugby match.

'Ipi lo problem?' yells one constable. Nightshift points. 'That man over there told me to break into the workshop to fetch him a jack.' The policeman looks momentarily confused. 'So? Why didn't you?' It is clear that the situation here is under control. A guy in a kilt is fixing a wheel. Four security guards are standing around, laughing. Some other guys are trying to fit the wrong-sized fanbelt on a broken-down kombi. A petrol station attendant is not saying a thing.

No arrest will be made, no dockets will be opened. Still, at half past one on a Sunday morning, it is a situation worth perusing. 'Jeez,' says a plainclothes policeman, staring at the rim and axle of the car that didn't make it back to base by midnight. 'That's exactly what happened to my Alfa.'

The spare is in place now. The nuts are fastened tight. The driver is ready to make up for misplaced time. No, he's not. He's locked the keys in the boot. He clambers in the back, punches some hardboard out of the way, and rolls into the driver's seat. Ignition. This is not a good idea.

'Listen, oke. I don't think it's a very good idea to...'

He's moving. Groan of metal, slither of vulcanised rubber. Ten metres. He's at the stop-street. He's turning left. Very slowly, tugging at the wheel like a ship's captain in a storm. That does not sound good. Any second now, that shear of jagged metal is going to... blam. In the distance, the sound of a freight-train ironing out speedbumps. This time, uphill. It is our civic duty to catch up with this guy and tow him, and his vehicle, back to camp. But none of the fanbelts fit.

We're going to have to leave the kombi here overnight, and get a lift home with the Good Samaritan. It's two o'clock. We're waiting at the robots. There's a car in the next lane. In the back seat, hunched over and crammed on top of each other, half a dozen teenagers, probably on their way back from a party. In the front seat, fast asleep: the guy with the kilt.

Listen, oke. Next time you get the urge to go jolling in a military vehicle, here's a simple word of advice. Take a tank. Oh, and one more thing. If you're going to go around in a kilt, always be sure to carry a spare pair of pantihose.

CARRY ON UP THE JUNTA

Coming in to land at KD Matanzima international airport, gateway to the Republic of Transkei, I see pink and green huts, a muddy brown river, and hillocks that rise from the earth like the bare knuckles of a clenched fist. Here and there, a cow or sheep tugs at the scratchy yellow turf, and the skeletons of motorcars rust in peace in the valleys.

I clear Customs & Immigration — in the dwindling days of the homeland system, the rituals of sovereignty are diligently observed — and I head down the highway to Umtata. An XA driver bears down on me, hooter blaring and lights flashing, and I selflessly grit my teeth to allow him to overtake on the solid white line.

Someone had warned me that this is how people drive in the Transkei, where traffic officers are almost as rare as foot-soldiers of the Azanian People's Liberation Army. So I drive a little faster myself. I don't want to be mistaken for a tourist, and in any case, I more or less have an appointment to see the Chairman of the Military Council, Major-General Harrington Bantubonke Holomisa.

'Just phone when you get here,' the General had instructed. 'I can't say what time I will be in or out. I have pressing constitutional matters to attend to.'

I phone from the Holiday Inn. The Captain puts me through to the General. 'Hello,' he says. 'This is the General.' There is a brief rustling of papers as he checks his schedule, and then he says, 'OK. You can come now.'

The voice, despite its mellow, malted quality, makes me think of a lit fuse, so I hurry down to the Botha Sigcau Building after asking the General for directions.

Like the airport, the home of the Transkei Government has retained the names of yesterday's despots, for General Bantu Holomisa has had other priorities on his agenda since moving on to the 11th floor after the bloodless military coup of December 31, 1987. But it doesn't really make much difference.

Whatever you want to call the building, it is still impossible to find parking within a block of the entrance on a mid-winter Monday morning. I drive around for a while, dodging minibus taxis and waBenzis, eyes peeled for parking as I try to keep count of the number of times One Settler equals One Bullet on the spray-painted walls of downtown Umtata.

I give up when I reach the Tourist Information office, where the equation has been whittled right down to the bone: 'Kill A White A Day'. Ah. I park on a yellow line outside the Department of Posts and Telecommunications, following the precedent of several other civilian XA vehicles, and I run in the general direction of Leeds Street.

There is a mild air of shellshock about the Botha Sigcau Building. The Transkei flag weather-stained and fraying, the yellow walls flecked with grime, the balcony railing buckled and blown apart in the middle. Inside, the place feels like a university dorm on the day after exams.

Shrieking kids run up and down the lobby, civil servants dash to and from the lifts, soldiers and brown-uniformed policemen chat idly on the fringes. I pass a cursory security check, state my business, and catch the non-stop lift to the 11th floor.

In the carpeted, wood-panelled corridor, a man in a shiny blue suit catches my eye, and he stops, spins around, and takes friendly aim with a loaded index finger. It is the

General. He is 38 years old, young for the leader of a nation, not so young for the leader of an army.

He wears his civilian suit with the stately elegance of an emperor, and his black slip-ons bounce the sunshine from the window as he sits back in a wine-red leather chair. His jacket is buttoned in the middle, and he slips his right hand inside it, like Napoleon Bonaparte.

I ask the General about the security situation in Transkei, particularly with regard to settlers in transit. In the last few months alone, at least seven people, some lured by the rugged isolation of the coastline, some on business in the interior, have been brutally murdered by unknown assailants in the territory under General Holomisa's control.

Two brothers on a fishing trip were machine-gunned by men in black leather on the road to Port St Johns. An accountant from East London was stabbed, mutilated, and dumped in a forest near Umtata. A Japanese tourist was bludgeoned with a crowbar on a beach near the Wild Coast Sun.

The Department of Foreign Affairs and the South African Embassy in Umtata have advised South Africans to avoid travelling through the Transkei unless absolutely necessary. Are things really that bad? A look of surprise crosses the General's face.

'You are here,' he says, 'and you are from Johannesburg. You will have to assess the safety of the situation for yourself.' He is not a callous man; merely a pragmatist.

'Of course, it has affected our tourism. But the campaign against us had been led by the South African Government, through its Ambassador here, as well as the security forces. Statements have been issued. You find that if someone is killed here, and someone else is shot between Johannesburg and Vanderbijlpark, then the Transkei incident must be reported as a serious issue.'

The General shrugs broad shoulders — he used to play wing for the Transkei National Rugby Squad — and uses one of his favourite phrases. 'Hard luck. It's up to the individual tourist to decide whether to come here or not. I can't force anyone.'

Sitting here in the office of the Head of State, with his ankles crossed, his hands in his pockets, and a mischievous grin lighting up his face, General Bantu Holomisa looks like a schoolkid who has casually taken control of the head-master's office. In reality, that would have been the furthest thing from his mind.

The son of a headman of the AmaHegebe tribe, Holomisa was Vice-Head Prefect and Rugby Captain at school, and when he made his big career switch from post office technician's assistant to professional soldier, he carried the Sword of Honour at his passing-out parade and was promoted from Second Lieutenant to Major-General in less than ten years.

He is amiable, engaging, almost disarmingly accessible, but for all his egalitarian bonhomie, he never allows himself to forget who or what he is. A leader of men. A close associate of the General tells me, 'He is very aware of the fact that he is the Chief's son. He feels he is nobility, and deserves to be treated as such.'

Aside from the military bearing, the outward signs are the General's 'exquisite taste' in clothes — the tailored silk shirts and the pocket handkerchiefs — and his 'snobbish fondness' for classical music of the Italian School.

So, while he is often seen jogging through Umtata with a Walkman on his hip, he is not listening to pop music or mbaqanga; he is glued to Pavarotti. But never mind the music.

I ask the General whether, in the light of the attempted coup of 1990, the mini-mutiny of 1992, and the assassination of his close friend Chris Hani, he has ever felt the need to reassess his personal security. Perhaps replace the Walkman with a pistol. After all, he is the head of the junta. The General twists his lips into a lemon-sour expression.

'No. I still drive alone. My own BMW. I must rely on the intelligence. Sometimes, I see my bodyguards moving closer to me on a particular day, as if someone has told them something. But I don't want to know. I don't want to hear, "General! General! There are people who are plotting to attack you!" If that is the case, see to it that it doesn't happen. You mustn't come to me with all your crap stories. I'm too busy!'

The General rollicks with laughter, and it is almost possible to believe him. But someone else who has had close dealings with the General warns me: 'He is a bright and immensely charming character. But you have to remember that he is a military dictator. And a terribly arrogant and paranoid one, too. He believes that the whole world is plotting and conspiring against him.'

Certainly, the General has accused the South African Government of everything from economic sabotage to attempted assassination, and even if it is just filibustering, it has had the unmistakable effect of endearing the man to his people. Alone among the unelected homeland leaders, the General is seen to be on the side of the Struggle, although he has been careful not to choose his side too clearly. He gets a kick out of non-commitment.

'At grassroots level, people are always saying, "Holomisa is ours!" He's PAC. No, he's ANC. No, he is fighting for us all. The fact is, I do not belong to any political party. I am a soldier. You know, I watch the politicians at these conferences, and their constituents shout at them, "Comrade! Where did you get the mandate to do that?"

'But I don't like those politics. As a leader, you can't always phone everyone before you make a decision. People will say it is because I come from a family of dictators, but I believe if you are appointed to lead, you must lead. That's the school I grew up in.'

Still, people are saying, at grasstop level, that this alone makes the General an ideal candidate for the post of Minister of Defence or Chief of the SADF in the first post-Apartheid dispensation. The General fobs off the suggestion, but it takes him all the way back to his Staff Course in Revolutionary Warfare at the Army College in Pretoria in 1984, when the military was one of the few truly multiracial areas of South African society.

'There was this big Colonel from the Orange Free State, and he used to say to me, "Ja, Bantu, wat weet jy, jy is maar net 'n kaffer van die Transkei se Weermag af." I like making those kind of jokes, so I would tell him not to worry, because in ten years' time, the Army would be run by blacks. The funny thing is, I didn't really believe it either.'

At lunchtime in the streets of Umtata, I assess the safety of the situation for myself. There are hardly enough whites around to meet the daily quota of the person who wrote the slogan on the wall of the Tourist Information office, but there is not the slightest hint of tension or hostility in the air. It is not like Johannesburg at all. Here, you only have to stand on a street corner for a few seconds, and someone will come along and call you 'friend'.

'Tell me, friend,' says the man in the pin-striped suit, 'do you really think this is fair? All these people . . . and just one man. Surely it is only right that he must pack up and go.'

We are standing outside the offices of the Department of Education, watching a few hundred schoolteachers and other interested parties who have gathered to demand the resignation of Mr Kakudi, the Minister. 'Kakudi, You Must Retire and Rest In Peace.'

It is a sit-in strike, although some people are taking turns to toyi-toyi inside the candy-striped police cordon. A man with a megaphone pressed too close to his lips is making muffled demands from the balcony, but he is drowned out by the buzzing of a TDF helicopter in the lazy winter sunshine. People shout, jeer, wave sticks in the air. I agree. Mr Kakudi must pack up and go.

I take a drive out to the South African Embassy, which is conveniently located on the road to the airport. You can't miss it; it's the only Embassy in town. It is a big brick fortress, on a rocky outcrop splashed with red-hot pokers, and once you are on the right side of the razor-wire, you are rewarded with a sweeping vista of the Drakensberg range beyond the dry Transkei hillocks. On a clear day you can see South Africa.

The Ambassador, Horace van Rensburg, grew up in Transkei, and he tells me the grass used to be so green, 'it would hurt your eyes'. He remembers that when you went on holiday, you would leave your front door wide open, in case friends or neighbours came around and wanted to make themselves a pot of tea. Times have changed.

For Transkeians and South Africans alike, the Ambassador's door is always open, but the gates of the embassy have been fortified and double-bolted since the day some 3 000 uninvited guests forced their way on to South African sovereign territory in protest at the assassination of Chris Hani.

The Ambassador, who used to be Progressive Federal Party MP for Bryanston, says it is important to point out that he has 'enjoyed every minute' of his posting in Umtata.

'It has been very challenging, and also difficult on occasion, because of the heightened political atmosphere here. But this is a wonderful country. The potential for tourism, agriculture, industry is enormous. Do you know that the Transkei is bigger than Taiwan? It has better weather than Taiwan. Of course, Taiwan has the largest foreign exchange reserves in the world. But there is absolutely no reason, other than the motivation of the people themselves, why the Transkei shouldn't be a very successful and prosperous country.'

Strolling through the grounds of the embassy, the Ambassador stops, looks up, and points out a 9mm bullet-hole in a security grille over a window. The paint has been chipped, and the metal dented like putty.

And over here, on the tarmac, a thin, dark petrol stain, the contents of a Molotov Cocktail a woman was about to throw before she lost her footing and slipped off the embankment. And over there, the trampled, uprooted, deflowered remains of the Embassy Gardens. But there have been other difficult days.

On one occasion, when passage was blocked off by barricades of blazing car-tyres, a small knot of protesters — the Ambassador battles to recall the reason for the protest —

made their way up to the embassy's ornamental fish-pond. There, having trashed the pump, they reached into the water, scooped up the goldfish, and angrily bit their heads off.

The goldfish have not been replaced. But in the garden, a woman kneels to tend a rosebush, and cross-piled bags of organic fertiliser wait to be spread over the soil. One day, the garden will bloom again, and this place will no longer be an embassy.

On the road back to the city, I notice a profusion of what people sometimes call the 'National Flower' of the Transkei: paper bags. Littering has been one of General Holomisa's main concerns since the day he took office, so I ask him how the campaign is going. Not bad, he says. 'The people are being conscientised. But they need assistance.'

And so the General has employed squads of pensioners to pick up rubbish in the city centre, and he has dispatched platoons of soldiers to patrol the verges of the N2 with rubbish-bags in their hands. The General's other main concern, and the one that prompted him to overthrow the regime of Prime Minister Stella Sigcau — 'The Lady' — has been to clean up the 18 departments of the Transkei Civil Service. Here, too, things are going well.

Already, three Commissions of Inquiry have been appointed to investigate alleged malpractice, abuse, and mismanagement in the Transkei Development Corporation, the Transkei Broadcasting Corporation, and the Transkei Road Transport Corporation. For the most part, the allegations do not make riveting reading.

There has been much abuse of PetroCards, travel allowances, encashment of vacation leave, and low-interest loans to senior executives. But as the Transkei prepares for reincorporation into South Africa, the parastatals have become, according to one Umtata official, 'fair game for looting', and the effect on the homeland's heavily subsidised economy has been ravaging.

The TDC, which once boasted assets of R1-billion, including the world's biggest chopstick factory, just outside Umtata, is now R18-million in the red. All development projects have been put into abeyance, and the staff of 1 000 have been served with retrenchment notices.

The new Civil Service tower, built at a cost of R65-million and known as 'The Skottel' for its hugely over-hanging helicopter-pad, remains conspicuously unoccupied at the entrance to town. Slowly but surely, the Transkei is making itself redundant. But there will always be a job for the General.

'I'm not looking for any rosy posts,' he insists. 'I've tasted power at the highest level, and I don't think I've misused it. OK, I'm open to correction on that one. But my aim in coming here was not to enrich myself. Not one property, not one business, have I ever bought. So when it comes, the reincorporation, it will make no difference to me, other than that I will be shoved back to the military as an ordinary soldier. No fanfare.'

The General is open to correction on that one. He is too young, too stroppy, too canny to retreat to barracks at this advanced stage of the campaign. He sinks back into his leather chair and slowly cracks his knuckles.

I ask him whether he regrets not having put his leadership to the test, as promised, by calling a General Election within a couple of years of assuming office. He stands up and gazes out of the window at the Umtata City Hall, with its colonial sandstone architecture and its pink granite plaque commemorating the official opening of the Umtata Sewerage Works in 1937.

'No,' he says. 'I don't regret it. Because there is no guarantee that I would even have won.'

The General turns around, his eyes widen, and he whispers through a cupped palm: 'Hey, who does this crazy young boy think he is? What makes him so jumpy? What's he going to do to us next?'

Only the General knows the answer, and he's not telling. Because right now, on the top floor of a decaying building in the heart of Umtata, he's just too busy laughing.

THE BIG GUAVA

On Saturday morning, when the people are driven to shop by the tightness of the day, I sit on my balcony and watch the one-legged tap-dancing evangelist pitching for money in the quadrangle below.

Five storeys high, at the intersection of President and Joubert in the epicentre of Johannesburg, I can hear every punch of his Bible, feel every click of his quivering sole. I can see over the shoulders of the crowd.

'God loves me!' says the one-legged tap-dancing evangelist, hopping like a stork to the edges of the laager. 'I am happy when I die.'

The clapping drains to a drizzle, and a few small coins spin on the pavement. The stork pecks them on the hop. He has a balance you can bank on, but he counts the coins on his crutches. I can count them from my balcony. The best of it is, I don't need to give him a cent.

Because I live in Johannesburg. And the one-legged tap-dancing evangelist comes with the territory. He comes with the rent. It's a bargain, really, living in the centre of Johannesburg.

You can get a good-sized one-bedroom apartment for a few hundred bucks a month, service included (they polish and shine the red corridor floors until you can see your soles in them). There are marble chessboard tiles in the foyer, lifts with concertina doors and a nice view of the frozen impala in the fountain in the park (free running water). Dion is right next door, Fontana just across the tramline.

There's just one snag, really. You have to live in the city, not the suburbs. The core, not the apple. The heart, not the ribcage. The inner skirts, the epicentre, the eye of the whirlpool: Johannesburg.

People live here. And not just on benches, not just in doorways. If you stop looking for gold in the paving cracks, and lift up your eyes to the washing lines, you will see the hidden evidence of life after closing time. The curtains, the potplants, the bicycles on the balconies, the lazy shadows that linger in the wake of the rush. I might even wave back.

An inner-city address, in almost any city in the world, is not only desirable but damn hard to get. To live in the city is to be plugged into its nerve, to be fused into its soul, to be part of its energy and throbbing. Suburbs are dead places with gardens. They are OK for dogs. I am talking about people.

People think there is something perverse about living in Johannesburg. It is too retrograde, too anti-social, too un-European. The city is an expedient place, to be tolerated, squeezed, and discarded after use. You wouldn't want to live there. People say: where do you live? I say: in

Johannesburg. People say: yes, but where in Johannesburg? I say: in Johannesburg, in Johannesburg.

Let me tell you why. It's lekker in Johannesburg. Things happen.

Cars backfire. Buildings implode. Guns shoot. I have learned to tell the difference. I think. The first bomb exploded like a fullstop at the end of a day that was leaden with tension and dark blue with the presence of policemen. They stood in pairs on street corners and people shielded their eyes and quickened their pace to work.

Their presence was not a comfort. It was an omen. It was as if they were daring something to happen. But nothing happened. It didn't even rain. The weight of the day lifted and people inched home as usual on the liquorice scribble of the motorways. This was what I liked best about living in town. Sitting on the balcony with a beer, watching the sun go down and the people get out.

That day, everyone down there looked limp and drained, like spent contraceptives. At 5.45 pm, the bomb went boom. I know, because I thought my watch had stopped. The bomb was a dull ache in the building next door. It was like having a tooth pulled: the relief was greater than the pain. It sounded like thunder. And there was thunder. The twilight sky burst with rain and wet police dogs barked in the shower of shop-glass.

I ran down the stairs (the lifts were out of order) and got there before all the other journalists. They were jealous, but it wasn't much of a story. One lady was led away, white-knuckled and weeping. Traffic officers wrapped the block in candy-striped tape to restrain ravenous cameramen and journalists. I refused to comment.

Suddenly, Mansfield House seemed a pretty safe place to be. We had looked into the eye of the storm, and the eye of the storm had blinked. Now we could all go back to sleep.

How do you sleep in town? You get used to it. The Rissik Street Post Office across the road is a national monument, but I have often wanted to blow it up. It has a clock that works. On many nights, I have slept 14 minutes at a time, burying my head under the pillow at the chimes. Midnight can kill you.

But I have grown to live by the clock, if not with it: I have become accustomed to carving out my life in quarter hours. I like the clock. The dull, sweet tolling of its bell anaesthetises the city's futile sense of urgency. Why rush? You may only live another 15 minutes.

Time passes. Johannesburg, the squatter-camp that became a city, turned 100 one year, and the City Council sent men around in trucks with hydraulic ladders. Late at night, and on Sunday mornings. They strung necklaces of coloured lights and centenary pendants in the spaces between buildings. It was nice of them, but people were trying to sleep. People had hangovers.

I do not mind the dustbinmen, who wear naartjie overalls and whistle and war-cry as they feed the belly of the monster-truck at 11 pm every night. I do not mind the little old man with the khaki jacket, who jangles keys and disembowels parking meters late every second night. I do not mind the electric blue wail of police sirens, or the guinea-pig squeal of frightened car alarms, or the thud, smash, and tinkle of shatterproof glass, because all of these things make me happy to be inside.

I mind people who sing. One day a man named Arthur Blessit came to live in the park with the frozen impala. Arthur

Blessit was an American. He had his cross to bear. It was an eternal life-size replica with training wheels on the upright, and it had gone around the world with Blessit in front.

Blessit himself was built like a cross, with grey hair and holy eyes and lots of grain and chisel. He seemed like a nice enough bloke, but he had disciples. They came from the suburbs. They had sleeping bags and flasks of coffee. They slept in the park for a week. That was OK, but they woke up too. Usually at three in the morning.

They clapped hands: 'Oh Jesus, I have promised, to serve you to the end, be thou forever near me, my master and my friend. Hallelujah! Ay-men.'

Arthur Blessit was in the park, blessing people, on the day the second bomb went off. I was inside, biting through a wholewheat cheese and chutney roll from the Bread and Butter Sandwich Company.

My first reaction was that it must have been something I ate. I ran to the balcony and stopped just in time. The park was hidden for a moment by the elastic flap of pigeon wings, arcing in a cloud in the aftershock. Lazy lunchtime people lying in the park shot on to their elbows; other people leaped over them like impala. The blast had come from the west.

A guy with a Betacam TV camera on his shoulder sprinted west with intent. Arthur Blessit was sitting on a bench with his cross behind him. His hands were on the heads of people who were kneeling. They didn't blink. They stayed there like rocks as the tide swirled around them.

Against my better instincts, I decided to stay inside and finish my roll. One heard about bombs: the first was just a magnet, the second was a sledgehammer. Then my better instincts said what the hell. I ran down the stairs (the lifts were out of order) and headed west. Many people were heading north and south and east, which made me wonder whether the blast hadn't been a backfire after all.

But there was candy-striped tape around the Wimpy Bar in Rissik Street. A man was walking around with his trouser leg in fringes below the knee. There was blood on the glass on the tarmac. A little old lady was pointing at a television cameraman and shouting at a traffic officer.

'I live exactly across the road! And that TV man was here even before I looked out of the window! What are you going to do about it?'

The cop flexed his fingers inside his elbow-length gloves. 'I'm sorry, lady. I just got here myself.'

There was a second bomb, but it was just a hollow rumble on the east side of town. I ate my roll. I began to wonder if it was worth living in town, living right on the head of the pressure cooker. Hell, yes: it just wasn't worth dying there.

There had been bombs in the dustbins. So they took away the dustbins. They ripped the yellow drums off robots and sealed the mouths of the bigger bins with metal plates. You couldn't throw away a limpet mine, but you had to walk around all day with a banana peel in your hand.

Johannesburg is a dirty town, but it outgrows its rubbish like a snake shedding its skin. You can learn to deal with it, once you remember that cockroaches have right of way. Cockroaches I don't mind; cockroaches don't try to sell you religion.

The Hare Krishna missionaries wear gold paint on their noses and silver on their tongues. They stand in the quadrangle and greet you sweetly and thrust paperback Bibles into your hands. If you have no money, they thrust them back and present you with a voucher for a free vegetarian meal instead. But there is no such thing as a free vegetarian meal. I'm afraid I regularly give the Hare Krishnas reason to be grateful for their serenity.

On other days, the Scientology Institute sets up a table and flogs religion in the guise of higher intellect. A guy who looks like a Scientology Institute salesman hands you a pamphlet stamped purple with Albert Einstein's face. YOU ONLY USE 10 PER CENT OF YOUR POTENTIAL.

The other 90 per cent is hidden in a book called Dianetics and a course which unlocks the Einstein in you. For a small fee. By the end of the day, the quadrangle is snowed under with Einstein's purple head and other people's footprints.

Old Joe tap-dances in the quadrangle every other lunchtime. He is the real thing, with two legs and white shoes and silver tongues click-clacking on the pavement. He is tall and thin, with bruises and yellow teeth: walking doesn't suit him. But he taps.

One day the metallic clatter of his tapping is blanketed by chants and the drumfire of running feet. From the balcony I glimpse a dark forest of fists. Old Joe carries on tapping, but his audience gets lost in the forest. A white car speeds the wrong way down the one-way; doors slam and men in suits rush out, holding down the flaps of their jackets.

They return, walking, not smiling. The man in the middle cuts away, his hands, knees, and elbows knifing as the crowd parts to let him through. There are cheers and ululations. Not from the men in suits. They circle the block and a yellow car empties more of them. Everything is out of frame now. I think of running down the stairs, but there are already too many people running.

The cutaway man runs back up the same street, twice as fast and twice as trapped. He trips and falls into the back of a red bakkie. The midday air is thick with car hooters and seething, and a dog with naked fangs is dragging a traffic cop by the leash. A big yellow bus with fencing on the windows lumbers at the tail of the dead snake of traffic. Men hang from the open doors with liquorice spears in their hands.

They get there. But they are the only action. People disperse. The dog's tail is wagging, its front paws are in the air. Old Joe carries on tapping.

These things happen in Johannesburg. It is a city. It tap dances all day on the knife-edge of violence; at night, it tiptoes. Guns go pokka-pokka and somewhere people scream. The clock chimes three. I could be dreaming. I wake up one Sunday morning and there is somebody lying in the park. Face-down. Policemen taking notes.

I am in the bath one Saturday afternoon when the lazy calm outside is dented by gunfire. When I get to the balcony (the doors are always open, just in case) there is a guy lying on the pavement and a man with a holster, crouching. These things are worth a paragraph in the next day's paper, but are they worth leaving town for?

I am waiting for a bus one night at the Van der Bijl bus terminus in the deep end of downtown. It is the end of the night as well as the end of the line, but you learn to trust the darkness. More people get mugged in the sharp stab of daylight. Anyway, I live in town. I am townwise.

A figure shifts and shuffles out of the heavy wrap of night. Bruised cheeks. Knife-scar, two fingers touching cut lips. 'Hello boss. You haven't got a cigarette for me?'

'Sorry, don't smoke.' Cool, easy, smiling. Waiting for the bus. Deep stare. 'You haven't got fifty cents for me?'

'Uhhh . . .' Thumb in money-pocket, feeling for silver among the paper, trying not to rustle, trying not to sweat. Here's twenty cents.

'Thanks boss.' A sudden slap on my wrist. Hey, what kind of soul handshake . . . My watch! Slap of feet on tarmac, fade to black. What the hell. Still got the clock.

People mug, people get mugged. It is easy to get melodramatic, easy to get paranoid, easy to get macho and blasé. Johannesburg is the kind of town where you run like crazy when someone you've never met says hello to you. Maybe you owe the guy money; maybe he'll take it anyway. After a while you stop saying hello. People are not only paranoid, people are broke.

It's tough living in town, but it's lekker. Especially when it's raining. Rain suits Johannesburg: a dark-grey suit with pinstripes, or navy-blue with silver threads at night. Far from making the place melancholy, rain lifts the lid off the pressure cooker and gives it room to breathe. To sigh: I look out of my window now and watch the low clouds floating on needles in the foglight, and the white sweep of headlamps on roads as black as rose petals, and the little red robot men dancing in the puddles, and the orange glow of wet stone buildings, and the sheets of rain dripping from the halo of a streetlamp.

In the daytime there are rainbows and umbrellas with legs: the oil blotches from cars turning left into President Street look like peacock feathers when you're five storeys high. Johannesburg is not a pretty city, but it's only as ugly as you make it.

I reckon it's OK. I sit here and watch the old Zulu watchman taking the landlady's toy pom for a walk in the park. The dog wears a little red jersey, the old Zulu wears big rings in his earlobes. I watch the girls with the fishnet stockings and the liver-red lipstick, waiting on the corner for the men in the Mercedes convertibles.

I watch the coalmen hauling coal down to the boiler in the cellar (free hot water!) and coming back up with empty sacks over their heads, like cowls. The white chessboard tiles are black with soot. I watch the men from the Traffic Department hooking their towaway truck to the bumpers of illegally parked cars. I watch the owners return. They never win.

On Saturday afternoons, I watch the Soweto Drum Majorettes swaying their hips and chewing gum to the echoing clatter of snare drums in the quadrangle below. I don't need to give them a cent. I watch the sun set over the City Hall. I never watch it rise. Town's lekker, man. But I'm leaving. Shit, you can't find parking anywhere.

OPINION

YOU'LL NEVER WIN A REVOLUTION
IF YOUR CLOTHES ARE REVOLTING

Flanked by soldiers wearing full-face balaclavas and cradling Army-issue submachine guns, a fugitive from justice declares war on the Government from his secret underground hideout. Isn't it romantic? The Rebel flag; the stolen arsenal; the videotaped call to arms and honour and the glory of the Revolution. Wow! The Revolution!

Workers downing tools and picking up hammers and spanners and lead pipes as they march on the citadel of the Government. Poets and artists kicking over statues. Politicians and judges kicking over statutes. Soldiers waving from the backs of cattletrucks. People singing and dancing in the city square.

Come on, everybody, let's revolt! Let's storm the ramparts! Let's... hang on a second. Is this the right Revolution we're talking about? Nope. It's the Right Revolution. Who do these guys think they are? How dare they presume to hijack the Revolution before it's even begun?

Listen, Piet 'Skiet' Rudolph, guerrilla leader on the run, commander-in-chief of the Orde Boerevolk, there are certain basic rules in this game, and one of them says you cannot proclaim a revolution from a position of privilege. You have to be downtrodden, dispossessed, disenfranchised, hungry, and fed-up. But all that is beside the point.

For the single most important rule is that you cannot proclaim a revolution, and you cannot expect to win the support of the people, unless you are properly dressed.

Now, as far as I can recall, Piet 'Skiet' Rudolph, in his secret underground hideout on the eight o'clock News, was wearing an open-necked nylon shirt and a mustard sports jacket with big buttons and flick-knife lapels. Forget it, Piet. History will not tolerate the unstylish Revolutionary. It's that simple.

If we take a random flip through the Great Revolutions of the last few centuries, what do we find, apart from mindless mob violence, mass delusion, and a sudden sharp increase in the gold price? What we find, baby, is a sense of style, an overwhelming awareness that fashion and ideology are flip-sides of the same freshly minted coin. Let's take a look at a few well-worn examples.

As everyone knows, the French Revolution of 1789 consisted of a bunch of peasants running around shouting about Liberty, Equality, and Fraternity, following which they set fire to historic buildings and hacked the heads off their superiors. Yet history has forgiven them, and all because they wore floppy conical hats, trousers rolled up to just below the knee, and football scarves in classic red, white, and blue.

If we move on to the Mexican Revolution of 1911, we find the rebel forces of Pancho Villa and Emiliano Zapata shooting at trains and pillaging villages in a bid to secure their freedom from the United States of America. On the fashion front we find criss-cross leather ammunition belts, wide-brimmed sombreros, moustaches, stubble, and Te-quila. Such a stylishly accessorised Revolution could hardly go wrong, which explains the electrified fencing along the Rio Grande, a desperate yet essential measure to keep the Americans from crossing the border.

*Why the Far Right failed to ignite the spark of a
People's Revolution*

The Bolshevik Revolution of 1917 offered little aside from greatcoats and bold splashes of red, but if we take a Long March forward to the Cultural Revolution in China during the Sixties, we find the first real stirrings of Communist fundamentalism as a popular fashion statement.

The Red Guards of Chairman Mao battered schoolteachers on the head with rifle-butts and set fire to copies of Mark Twain's Huckleberry Finn, but the student intellectuals of France and the psychedelic hippies of America saw Red, and fell blindly in love.

Andy Warhol churned out pink and purple screenprints of Chairman Mao's fat, smiling face, and everyone who could read Chinese went around quoting from the Little Red Book: 'A Revolution is not a dinner-party.' (What is it then, a brunch?)

But the point is, people are generally quite prepared to overlook little lapses in decorum, such as the burning of books and the bayoneting of political cartoonists, as long as the officers and soldiers of the People's Army look good on posters and in double-page fashion-spreads.

Hence, the continuing infatuation with Che Guevara's groovy beard and beret, the sunglasses of the Sandinistas, and the tassled, two-tone keffiyehs of the Palestinian Intifada. We all know what Pol Pot's Khmer Rouge were really like — after all, we saw the movie — but somehow, we find it hard to argue moral absolutes with a bunch of guys who look so cool in Rouge.

Listen, Piet 'Skiet' Rudolph, in your secret underground hideout, just keep on dressing like a civil servant at a Sunday afternoon braai in Bapsfontein. We prefer you that way. Honest.

THE BLANK SPACE ON THE T-SHIRT

Hey, you know what I really miss about the State of Emergency? (I'm talking about the big State of Emergency, not the limited edition in Natal.) I miss the blank spaces.

That's right, those elegant little areas of eloquent emptiness that told you all you didn't need to know about terror, repression, resistance, subversion, and the colour of naked newsprint.

Well, I used to think they were cool. They were white holes into which you could pour your most lurid visions of the world outside your double-bolted door and your burglar-barred window, and even if you got a few of the details wrong, at least you had the satisfaction of knowing it was all your own work.

It's like watching the Texas Chainsaw Massacre, and just at the point where Leatherface lifts his whining, buzzing chainsaw in the air . . . the projector blows a valve, the frame freezes, and the picture slowly burns up from the inside.

So you watch the rest of the movie in your head, and you get a lot more massacre for your money.

I started thinking about this the other day, when I drove down the freeway and zoomed past an enormous blank billboard. It was the only billboard I noticed, the only product I remembered: Nothing.

There is something very tantalising about emptiness, an elusive quality that somehow goes missing when you attempt to fit the void with reality. Let's look, for example, at Nelson Mandela.

Now, I remember when Nelson was just a blank space in the newspaper and the history books, leaving it up to you to mould and carve your own vision of the way he looked, thought and spoke. Of course, there were clues, but they were the problem. You focused on those old black-and-white pictures of the Scarlet Pimpernel, and you looked into those phrases from the transcript of his trial, and things just started getting out of hand.

So, when Nelson Mandela walked out of Pollsmoor on February 11, 1990, I thought: Great. Now he's going to say a few words.

After all, the guy was a lawyer, right? And he must have given some thought, in 27 years, to what he was going to say in his opening argument, right? Right.

This was going to be Neil Armstrong on the moon, Martin Luther King at the Washington monument, John Fitzgerald Kennedy in Berlin. This was going to be monumental.

Nelson Mandela said a few words. He put on his reading glasses, cleared his throat, and read a short paragraph about the continuation of the Armed Struggle. It sounded like he was talking about the continuation of the Public Roads maintenance programme by the Department of Public Works.

Then he spoke about Nationalisation, and it sounded like he was speaking about, well, Nationalisation.

Where was the fire, the passion, the poetry? Right there. In the blank spaces. It's been a while since then, and Nelson Mandela has spoken to the United Nations, and the American Congress, and film stars and baseball fans and trade union leaders and Yasser Arafat.

And the more you listen, the more you think about it, the more you have to admit that, well, you know — and hey, this is nothing personal, you understand — Nelson Mandela isn't such a red-hot orator after all.

He's more of a facilitator, a diplomat, an organisation man. He speaks slowly and without emotion, picking at his words like a vegetarian at a braaivleis.

You listen out for the quotes, the sound bites, the headlines, but somehow, they pass you by. Is this it? Is this the Collected Sayings of Nelson Mandela?

Look, let's be reasonable about this. Fundamentally, there's nothing wrong with humility and dignity and inner charisma and all that stuff. It's just that, so far, Nelson Mandela hasn't really said anything that would look good on the front of a T-shirt.

There's a big blank space there, waiting to be filled. Come to think of it, maybe I'll leave it that way. Just in case of Emergency.

GOODBYE ALBANIA, IT WAS NICE NOT KNOWING YOU

If you look hard enough, you can usually find it, somewhere on the edge of the map. Albania. It's that kind of place, distant, enigmatic, introverted. The Greta Garbo of nations, a gold mine for Trivial Pursuit compilers: What's the capital of Albania? Who's the president? What's the gross national product? Who cares?

Well, for a start, me.

I mean, we're talking about Albania, the most antisocial socialist republic in the world, a country that has consistently gone out of its way to offend friends and alienate people, whether they be socialist or communist or capitalist imperialist. In a world full of pragmatists and shifting political principles, Albania has always wanted to be alone, an island of inflexibility in a sea of ingratiating accommodation.

No frank and fruitful discussions for Albania's ambassadors, no cocktail-party photo opportunities, no sun-kissed solicitations of Western package tourists. No negotiations, no compromise, no perestroika. Nothing.

Just constructive disengagement, collective self-sufficiency, and rock-solid faith in the surrogate god, Josef Stalin.

Well, as they say in the history books, that's all history now, baby. Because something's going on in the People's Socialist Republic of Albania, and the place is never going to be the same.

We all know the story by now. Little murmurs of popular discontent. Thundering affirmations of the status quo. Whispered conversations on street corners. Loud denunciations of the counter-revolutionary conspiracy. The rattling of the embassy gates. The sit-ins. The frantic pleas by foreign ministers.

And then, the moment of weakness, the surprise humanitarian gesture: a handful of hastily arranged passports, stamped and delivered on the way to the airport.

This is really scary. We're living in a world where you can't even rely on Albania any more. Pretty soon, they'll be marching in the streets, unfurling their ethnic minority emblems and burning their Communist Party membership cards. Pretty soon, they'll be kicking down the statues of Josef Stalin.

Pretty soon, everybody will know exactly how to find the People's Socialist Republic of Albania on a map of the world.

Now, on the one hand, this is all very exciting, for justice and democracy shall shine their light in the heart of darkness, and the people of Albania will be free to order a

Big Mac and a Coke to go, and the citizens of other countries, even South Africa, will come in peace with travellers' cheques and cameras and MasterCards.

On the other hand, as the last outpost of the Evil Empire, Albania has a very clearly defined role to play in the global psychodrama, and we can't just have key players wandering in and out of character whenever it suits them.

We don't want subtlety and shading here, and nor do we want sudden twists in the plot.

We want absolutes, opposite poles of good and evil, and we want those poles to be anchored in bedrock, not quicksand.

Come on, Albania. We've given up on the USSR, and Bulgaria and Romania, and, quite frankly, we're not even going to mention the East Germans.

We're relying on you, Albania, to stand firm, to stand tall for Stalin, to turn your back on the temptations of Glasnost and the Eurodollar and the multiparty state.

You don't need that stuff, Albania. But we need you, like we need Dracula and the Bogeyman and the Teenage Mutant Ninja Turtles.

We need you, alone, to uphold the great and noble tradition of the International Communist Conspiracy. We need you to be brutal and reclusive and, well, Albanian, because that's the way we understand you, and that's the way we trust you.

Look at it this way. You've spent four gruelling decades trying to convince the Albanian people that you're right, and that Russia and China and America and the rest of the world are wrong.

Well, maybe you're right. But what if you're wrong?

Let's not put it to the test, Albania. Let's... no, hang on. It's already too late. You've bent under the strain. You're letting your people go. You're opening the borders. You're processing passports. You're letting in journalists. You're changing. And you can't go back now.

So goodbye, Albania, it was nice not knowing you. And welcome to the world.

WE'RE ALL GOING ON A PUBLIC HOLIDAY

It is, as I sit here staring blankly out of the window, trying hard to whip up the energy to get down to work, a very special day in the history of the new South Africa. It is a red-letter day, a day quite unlike any other. It is a Public Holiday. Don't ask me which one.

All that matters is that it is a Tuesday, and — hey! I've just caught another glimpse of red on my calendar for the week. Would you believe it? The Thursday is a Public Holiday as well. Don't ask me which one.

All that matters is that the Tuesday and the Thursday are officially out of the window, which means that we may as well take the Monday and the Friday as well. And the Wednesday. What's the point of going to work one day, and then not going, and then going, and then not going?

It would only confuse people, and studies show that confused people are the single leading cause of South Africa's appallingly low workplace productivity rate and stop-start economic growth pattern. Personally, I always find that you need a little space to clear your head after a well-deserved Public Holiday.

Going back to work without adequate preparation can be hazardous, particularly if you operate heavy machinery, drive a truck, or work for the Independent Electoral Commission. My point, ladies and gentlemen, is that we urgently need more Public Holidays in South Africa.

I know there are people out there, such as SACOB (the South African Chamber of Business), AHI (the Afrikaanse Handelsinstituut), and CAMAWUSA (the Calendar Manufacturers and Allied Workers Union of South Africa), who would argue that we already have more than enough Public Holidays in South Africa. But I would suggest that they take a couple of days off work, and pause to consider the facts.

Let's begin with Wednesday, April 27, 1994. One of the quietest days of the year. A day almost entirely free of crime, violence, political upheaval, and industrial unrest. And why? Because it was a Public Holiday. Same goes for Thursday, April 28, 1994. A day on which all South Africans, other than Eugene Terre'Blanche and a spokesman for SACOB, felt suffused by a strange glow of good neighbourliness and inner contentment. That's what Public Holidays do to you.

They have a special air of lassitude and mellow contemplation, an air of winter sunshine that makes you want to go fishing, or perhaps spend seven and a half hours standing in a queue. Indeed, if we'd only had more Public Holidays in South Africa, we wouldn't have had to hold an election in the first place. Now that we have, certain people have been standing up in public and demanding the abolition of all Public Holidays that might remind us of the 'Old South Africa'. What nonsense!

Now, more than ever, we need Public Holidays that remind us of the iniquities and injustices of the past, such as the colonisation of the Cape (April 6), the Battle of Blood River (December 16), and the Comrades Marathon (May 31). Rather than do away with these days, we should hold on to them in the true spirit of reconciliation, using them as the foundation for more and bigger Public Holidays that will unite South Africans across the cultural and political spectrum.

Unlike ordinary working days, which have an almost unlimited potential for sparking conflict among various sectors of the population, Public Holidays have a habit of bringing South Africans together by making sure they stay as far away from the workplace as possible. Of course, this does not apply to people who work behind the counter at video stores. What else is there to do on a Public Holiday in South Africa?

But to get back to the main argument, may I just point out that South Africa, as usual, is way behind the rest of the world when it comes to number of Public Holidays on calendar. According to my calculations, there are five months of the year in South Africa in which there are NO OFFICIAL PUBLIC HOLIDAYS AT ALL. Yet the rest of the world is full of them.

In November, for example, while we slave away without respite, the Americans celebrate 'Thanksgiving'. In February, while we toil without interval, the Japanese celebrate 'Setsubun' (Bean-Throwing Festival). In August, while we celebrate without rest, the Swedes celebrate 'Sour Herring Day'. And in England, almost every second day is a 'Bank Holiday', held for no other reason than to celebrate the fact that the banks are closed.

Well, I say it's time we caught up. A nation without Public Holidays, or without enough Public Holidays, is a nation without pride, a nation without history, a nation without heroes. Let's forget about this 'Public Works Programme' everyone keeps going on about, and let's turn our energies and initiative to a fully-fledged, all-inclusive 'Public Holidays Programme' instead.

But not today, please. It's a Public Holiday. Anyone out there have any idea when we're all supposed to go back to work?

MRS NUJOMA, YOUR CHEQUE IS IN THE POST

On assignment for Network in Namibia last week, Cliff Saunders took time off from his hectic schedule to pay a visit to Sam Nujoma's mother. Fortunately for her, she wasn't home. Unless she was in hiding in one of the scraggly huts on her humble abode which, as Cliff pointed out, was in stark contrast to the 'affluence and jetsetting lifestyle which her son so readily sports in public'.

Accompanied only by an entire platoon of South African reconnaissance commandos and a modest convoy of armoured cars, Cliff hopped off a Casspir, dodged a few of Sam Nujoma's mother's chickens and set off to interview the woman who had informed him that Mrs Nujoma was not in at the moment. She helped him with his inquiries.

'Does Sam Nujoma send money to his mother?' asked Cliff through an interpreter.

The woman shook her head.

'Why doesn't Sam Nujoma send money to his mother?' persisted Cliff, wearing a spotless safari waistcoat in stark contrast to the woman's oily rags. She shrugged her shoulders.

Then Cliff climbed into one of the armoured cars which the South African Defence Force so readily sports in public, and the convoy churned up dust in its continuing quest to track down relatives of Sam Nujoma who hadn't received a cheque in the post since the declaration of independence.

For his dedication to duty and his relentless determination to uncover a new angle in the Namibian conflict, Cliff Saunders deserves to be nominated for an Artes in the category of Best Contribution to a Public Affairs Programme. Should this be the case, Cliff would be well advised to make like Sam Nujoma's mother and not be available for the occasion.

For on a sliding scale of acceptable evils, hiding away in a hut in Okandjero must surely be preferable to sporting an Artes award in public.

This theorem was proven beyond all doubt on Saturday night, when the SABC crossed over to the SABC for a live transmission of the award ceremony to end all award ceremonies. We should be so lucky.

Standing in the foyer of a studio at Auckland Park, Artes non-nominee Eben Engelbrecht identified important guests ('And here comes the Minister in the Office of the State President entrusted with Information, Broadcasting Services, and the Film Industry, Mr Stoffel van der Merwe') and filled us in on what was going to happen in a few feverish minutes from now.

'In Studio Five, technicians are feverishly preparing for the countdown ... seating for several hundred people has been arranged on the studio floor ... those lucky enough to have been invited will witness a spectacular variety show as well as see South Africa's top television performers being awarded the sought-after Artes ...'

It sounded unmissable, especially the bit about Stoffel van der Merwe sitting on the studio floor. The reality is too tedious to recount, but suffice to say that this year's Artes ceremony at least solved the nagging conundrum of how exactly the SABC managed to make a net profit of R53,8-million in the last financial year.

Easy. They made the money by cutting down on the budget for this year's Artes ceremony. They did away with the rainbow smoke and the girls in feathers and left us with a bunch of boys mincing mercilessly in bondage gear to canned Michael Jackson. They did away with the slick lighting and nifty camera cutaways and left us with blurred bits of vaguely famous people in the dark.

They did away with space-age décor and left us with a giant revolving lobster claw and the kind of mock-velvet wallpaper normally found in the lavatories of newly renovated one-star hotels in Boksburg.

The only thing they didn't do away with was the public transmission of the Artes Award ceremony.

Perhaps they would like to give this some thought before next year's ceremony. Otherwise I'm going to grab myself a cup of coffee. In Okandjero.

FILTH, SMUT, AND SEX WITH JOHN BISHOP

Sex and violence and drugs and dancing and topless bathing and escort agencies and blasphemy and sedition were all that it took to lure me away from the airbrushed centrefold of Bunny Girl when Network announced an in-depth investigation of the moral decay of the nation on TV1 last week.

Up to that point, the News had been nothing much to write to the Minister of Home Affairs about. Four South African soldiers had been killed in action in Angola, the Official Opposition had submitted an amendment bill to Parliament in order to facilitate a more effective implementation of the Group Areas Act, a Parliamentary Commission of Inquiry had been convened to investigate alleged abuses of Parliamentary letterheads for party political purposes, and the bodies of ten women who had been raped and strangled had been discovered in Klerksdorp.

The reason this discovery was not as newsworthy as the quarter-finals of the American Presidential election or the reinstatement of the Honourable Amichand Rajbansi as leader of the National People's Party was simple. The women were black.

So I carried on leering at Bunny Girl until the voice of John Bishop, jaunty yet grave, alerted me to the government's displeasure at the rising tide of smut and scum in our society, including the SABC. But at least the SABC was doing something about it. Gillian van Houten stopped people in the street and asked them about their morals. 'There aren't any morals in society,' said a lady with grey hair. 'The morals in South Africa are very, very low,' said a black man. 'Censorship in South Africa is a vunderful ting,' said a fat man.

People with very low morals gyrated under throbbing strobe lights and discarded their bikini tops and stuck dirty needles into their pale tattooed wrists. The Director of Publications listed a few of the undesirable things in life: 'Things which are indecent, obscene, offensive, harmful, blasphemous, and prejudicial to the good order'.

It was clear that censorship was therefore the only not undesirable thing in life. The camera pounced on a big word in a bookshop where undesirable persons browsed. SEX. Having swallowed that word whole, the camera snacked on VIOLENCE and leaped with relish on FILMS. John Bishop, reporting from the Low Morals desk of the SABC, picked up his phone and said he was going to call an escort agency. In order to protect his identity, he wore thick black bifocals and adopted the accent of a Scotland Yard detective pretending to be an East End taxi-driver.

'Allo,' said Inspector Bishop, 'izzat the hescort hagency?' Distant fuzzy squeals confirmed his suspicions. In common with every intrepid television presenter who has struggled to maintain a dynamic visual presence with a thick lug of plastic glued to his ear, Bishop frowned at the camera, chewed his lips, nodded, stared at the opposite wall, and wrote things down with unnecessary emphasis. Thirty-five to forty girls were available to spend the night with John Bishop for a fee of R50 an hour and R200 to the agency. 'Fanks a lot,' said Bishop, gently replacing the receiver on his way back to the studio.

There he faced a panel of experts who were deeply concerned for diametrically opposed reasons. But first he confirmed the call. 'That was a genuine call, there was someone at the other end offering me sex for money. Perhaps we can take that up a little later in this discussion.'

Sadly, there wasn't time. The director of United Christian Action of South Africa, waving his pocket Bible in the air, said it was unfortunate that the government had chosen to approach the issue of censorship from the perspective of the reasonable man, when 74 per cent of the population consisted of Christians. The serene Father in the velvet robe said trying to cure society's evils with censorship was like trying to cure a brain tumour with an aspirin. The arts editor of the Sunday Times said he would be interested to know the exact location of the corner cafés that openly stocked pornography to corrupt the minds of innocent children.

Me too. Until then, for the sheer perversity of its entertainment value, and for the diligent, enthusiastically undocumented manner in which it turned a pimple into a molehill, this edition of Network is hereby declared Not Undesirable. But only until the next edition of Bunny Girl.

TUNE IN, TURN ON, BURN OUT

Beaming into TV1 by remote control on Sunday, I arrived just in time to see hordes of Zulu warriors waving their assegais and whacking their shields as they war-danced their way out of a football stadium.

'They came in their thousands,' intoned the epic voice of Cliff Saunders, 'and then they left.' One could hardly blame them, for this was the tail-end of yet another Cliff Saunders investigation into why thousands of black people oppose mandatory economic sanctions and support Cliff Saunders. Suddenly, for no logical reason, other than the sight of Cliff Saunders, I felt irritated, run down, and short of patience.

'Are you easily irritated?' queried Gillian van Houten, as I kicked the cat and gnashed my teeth on the remote control. 'Do you often feel run down? Are you short of patience? Then you could be a potential victim of...executive burnout.'

Peak hour commuters blared hooters, traffic cops waved Mickey Mouse gloves, computer screens flickered falling share prices, stockbrokers shouted at each other. The message was as clear as a migraine. In today's fast-moving, high-pressured, teeth-clenching society, we were all potential victims of a Sunday night Carole Charlewood documentary on executive burnout.

A roadmap of the human body filled the screen, with the relevant executive bits labelled and arrowed for easy reference, as long as your nose was no more than two centimetres away from the screen. 'Pituitary.' 'Hypothalamus.' 'Catecholamines.' Utterly exhausted from the strain of reading the small print, I slunk back to my seat while an irritatingly serene woman from the South African Health Foundation outlined the danger signals of executive burnout.

'The person may experience a sense of feeling tired.' I began to experience a sense of yawning uncontrollably. 'He may frequently be late for appointments.' Sorry I missed the beginning of your documentary on Zulu attitudes to sanctions, Cliff. 'He may be subject to many minor irritations, like losing car keys.' I experienced a sense of being unable to remember where I had put the remote control. 'He may feel a tremendous resentment towards everybody.'

Suddenly, I caught a glimpse of Reeva Forman, cosmetics empress and Businesswoman of the Year, driving down life's highway with one hand on her car telephone and one hand on the wheel of her lipstick-red Alfa Romeo. Then she was sitting behind her desk wearing Alfa Romeo-red lipstick and talking to Carole Charlewood, who was wearing a Reeva-red dress on the other side of a bowl of rose-red roses.

'When you're faced with a crisis, as we are from time to time,' beamed Reeva, 'one tends to panic.' She frowned. 'This leads to executive stress.' She smiled. 'But I'm trying to build up the habit pattern of controlling that panic reaction.' She gritted her teeth. They were smudged with lipstick.

In a stress management gymnasium, burned-out executives had their beer bellies measured with calipers. They ran on the spot and cycled on the spot and rowed on the spot. A sports doctor on the spot said the best kind of exercise was the kind that got your heart rate up and made you breathe heavily and sweat. This also sounded like the best way to get executive burnout, which Carole Charlewood was in no immediate danger of doing.

She interviewed a woman about food over breakfast at a health farm, while burned-out executives clinked spoons and squelched grapefruit segments in the background. Then she interviewed a Consultant in Organisational Communication in a garden with purple flowers. 'If you can learn to communicate with yourself, you can reach out to other people and ask them for help.'

I communicated with myself for a while, and then, almost miraculously, I found what I was looking for. The remote control. Goodnight.

RELAX, EVERYBODY, IT'S JUST ANOTHER STATE OF EMERGENCY

On the eve of the declaration of the new improved State of Emergency on Thursday, a familiar old face popped up from nowhere to say a few words about truth and decency on the eight o'clock News. Old Michael de Morgan, who used to read the news on TV1 before his transfer to the diplomatic corps in London, had come to justify his new calling by casting doubt on the professional integrity of a rival television station.

The British Broadcasting Corporation, we were informed, had screened a documentary the previous night on black children who claimed they had been tortured in detention by members of the South African Police. Michael de Morgan had seen the documentary. All we were allowed to see was Michael de Morgan.

There was something disconcerting about the way he conscientiously avoided looking at the camera, but it soon became clear that he had not come to read the news, but to make it. Smiling diplomatically under his distinguished mop of chrome, de Morgan revealed with an air of casual triumph that one of the allegedly tortured children had clearly been reading from prepared notes while being interviewed by the BBC.

'He kept glancing down, like this,' said de Morgan, glancing down like that. The point of this revelation was unclear, coming as it did from a man whose job at the SABC consisted almost entirely of reading from prepared notes on an electronic autocue. It must have been torture. Still, it was nice to see de Morgan once again occupying his customary timeslot, even if it was only for a few minutes via satellite from the real world.

Indeed, no SABC newsreader has ever managed to introduce an emergency with quite the same degree of drowsy warmth and distinguished complacency as de Morgan, although Clarence Keyter tried hard on Friday night. Echoing the official announcement of the return of the son of the State of Emergency, he nevertheless managed to stay awake against a background of soothing blue washes upon which the logo NOODTOESTAND lingered like a yawn.

Then the scene switched to the Houses of Parliament, where emergency correspondent Riaan Nel read extracts from the Government Gazette against a background of the Government Gazette. To foil people who were watching with the sound off, extracts from the Government Gazette appeared in large print on the screen, following which a photograph of the State President appeared from out of the blue of the NOODTOESTAND. This was replaced by the multiracial shield of the Bureau for Information, which had some good news: More than 90 per cent of black local authorities were functioning normally.

And some bad news. Incidents of terror, according to a soothing orange bar graph, had risen from 44 in 1984 to 234 in 1987, with a parallel increase in the number of Bureau for Information bar graphs. The revolutionary climate had not yet been brought under control. The news was a different matter. Four minutes. That was all the SABC could squeeze out of the renewal and extension of the State of Emergency for the third year in a row. No interviews; no comment; no analysis. No emergency. Well, a little one.

Was it fair? Was it just? Was it the decent thing to do? After the News and the Sport and the Money and the Weather, Clarence Keyter popped the questions to a member of South Africa's independent judiciary. Advocate Charles van der Walt, wearing a walrus moustache and an expression of smug condescension, assured Keyter and the nation that the State of Emergency was not only kosher, but completely compatible with the interests of democracy.

'The state has a duty to weigh the interests of the public against the interests of the individual,' testified the chief advocate of the State of Emergency, pausing only to caution the media that they could not demand any particular right without acknowledging their responsibility not to infringe on the rights of others.

'The State of Emergency must be seen in the light that all South Africans are striving towards normality, stability, development and progress in their daily lives.'

Until the next State of Emergency, then, keep striving.

THE LADY WHO WENT ON A DAY-TRIP TO HEAVEN

The uncontested highlight of the week's viewing was an interview with a woman who had died and gone to heaven for 28 minutes, and was now touring South Africa to promote a book on her travels.

'Heaven is a country as real as South Africa,' said Betty Malz, which made one a little alarmed at the prospect of hell.

Malz was a guest on the first edition of the new religious affairs programme, Lifestyle, which you can catch at high noon every second Sunday.

Co-host Wendy Millin, newly permed and radiant with spiritual rebirth in a violet sarong, said that we would be meeting some fascinating people and probing some challenging situations. Amen. Then we were introduced to Ken Hardy, who introduced us to 'a woman who has had two bites of the cherry in so far as she is now living her second earth-life. You see, she has already died once ...'

Betty Malz, an American, was wearing cherry lipstick and eyeshadow in the tone of funeral parlour purple that seems to dominate the décor of every SABC religious programme.

Malz began her story. It was a very long one. Being a person who had already died once, she was clearly possessed of an infinite concept of studio time.

'Appendicitis and peritonitis... serious vaginal infection caused by too much sun... mass of gangrene the size of a man's head... I had a bowel block for four days ... at the age of 13 I received Jesus... I knew that eternity was forever...'

Ken Hardy ummed and shuffled and hacked in a remarkably restrained attempt to interrupt the flow of eternity. 'Uh, Betty,' he croaked at length, 'can we move to the time when you actually died...'

Malz lifted her eyes to the spotlights. 'It was like... ' Sequins of glitter danced on the smudges of her eyeshadow. 'Like... ' Her diamond necklace smiled like teeth. Her teeth smiled like diamonds. '... Like being on a roller coaster in Disneyland.'

This was certainly enough to put you off Disneyland for life, if not for death, but what about heaven? Was it like a Hollywood amusement park too?

'It was beautiful... it was like forever spring... I heard the voice of a tenor I knew in Dallas. I began to sing in high sweet tones with the masses... light reflected down a golden boulevard... people were building...'

Malz's descriptions were vivid, but they made one wonder whether she had gotten on the right roller coaster. Ken Hardy also had his doubts: 'Betty, why did you leave? It sounds tremendous there.'

The camera cut to a pair of saffron-robed skinheads in the studio audience. 'Being a newspaper columnist and a writer of four books, I wanted to write and tell people how real it is . . . '

Things began to get even more real. Once Malz had been excused from heaven on the grounds of being a newspaper columnist, she found herself back in hospital, where she looked out the window and saw a black man carrying a case of 7-Up on his shoulder.

Then she knew she was alive again. 'I loved that black man so much, I woulda jumped out the window and hugged him. All racial prejudice was gone.'

There were some questions from the studio audience. Beau Brummel, the nudist (dressed for the occasion), wanted to know whether Malz had been financed to come to this country to sell Jesus for money.

Another man requested further details on the topography and natural attractions of heaven. 'I was 28 minutes in a place so awesome,' demurred Malz. 'I didn't see a whole lot there.'

Indeed, Malz's book is entitled My Glimpse of Eternity. Watching her on a scorching hot Sunday was mine.

ACKNOWLEDGEMENTS

Small print department: The author (that is to say, me) wishes to express his fulsome gratitude to the editors of the following newspapers and magazines, for their kind permission to reproduce the articles in this collection.

Thanks guys.

Marilyn Hattingh, Editor-in-Chief, Style magazine

Claudia Boffard, Editorial Director, Longevity magazine

Jane Raphaely, Editor and Publisher, Cosmopolitan magazine

Christina Pretorius, Editor, Flying Springbok

Denis Beckett, Editor-at-Large, Frontline magazine

Michael Wang, Editor-in-Charge, The Motorist

Anton Harber, 'Fat Editor', Weekly Mail

Chris Marais, 'The Ed', Living magazine

Shelagh Cameron-Dow, Editor, Tomorrow magazine